W9-BCL-596

CrochetWear

LEISURE ARTS, INC.
Little Rock, Arkansas

EDITORIAL STAFF
EDITOR-IN-CHIEF: Susan White Sullivan
KNIT AND CROCHET PUBLICATIONS DIRECTOR: Debra Nettles
SPECIAL PROJECTS DIRECTOR: Susan Frantz Wiles
SENIOR PREPRESS DIRECTOR: Mark Hawkins
ART PUBLICATIONS DIRECTOR: Rhonda Shelby
ART CATEGORY MANAGER: Lora Puls
SENIOR GRAPHIC ARTIST: Katherine Laughlin
PRODUCTION ARTIST: Janie Wright
EDITORIAL WRITER: Susan McManus Johnson
CONTRIBUTING TECHNICAL ASSOCIATE: Joan Beebe
IMAGING TECHNICIANS: Brian Hall, Stephanie Johnson,
and Mark R. Potter
PUBLISHING SYSTEMS ADMINISTRATOR: Becky Riddle
PUBLISHING SYSTEMS ASSISTANTS: Clint Hanson and John Rose

BUSINESS STAFF
VICE PRESIDENT AND CHIEF OPERATIONS OFFICER:
Tom Siebenmorgen
DIRECTOR OF FINANCE AND ADMINISTRATION:
Laticia Mull Dittrich
VICE PRESIDENT, SALES AND MARKETING:
Pam Stebbins
NATIONAL ACCOUNTS DIRECTOR: Martha Adams
SALES AND SERVICES DIRECTOR: Margaret Reinold
INFORMATION TECHNOLOGY DIRECTOR:
Hermine Linz
CONTROLLER: Francis Caple
VICE PRESIDENT, OPERATIONS: Jim Dittrich
COMPTROLLER, OPERATIONS: Rob Thieme
RETAIL CUSTOMER SERVICE MANAGER:
Stan Raynor
PRINT PRODUCTION MANAGER: Fred F. Pruss

*Our special thanks go to Jack Deutsch for photography,
Greg Clark for hair and makeup,
and Laura Maffeo for photostyling.*

Copyright © 2010 by Leisure Arts, Inc. This publication is protected under federal
copyright laws. Reproduction of this publication or any other Leisure Arts publication,
including publications which are out of print, is prohibited unless specifically authorized.
This includes, but is not limited to, any form of reproduction or distribution on or through
the Internet, including posting, scanning or e-mail transmission. We have made every
effort to ensure that these instructions are accurate and complete. We cannot, however,
be responsible for human error, typographical mistakes, or variations in individual work.

Library of Congress Control Number: 2009935747
ISBN-13: 978-1-60140-125-0
ISBN-10: 1-60140-125-6

10 9 8 7 6 5 4 3 2 1

CONTENTS

Catch the upbeat, offbeat, Big Apple beat of these original fashions by New York City designer Ann Regis! With each crochet pattern, the savvy urbanite shares her thoughts, tips, and favorite quotes on fashion. The 25 stylish designs include a variety of separates and accessories, and they offer plenty of excitement for crocheters of all skill levels. Let Ann's uncommon approach to crochet and her Five-Boroughs inspiration cast a new light on what you can achieve with this timeless art!

JACKETS

When you're dressing for style, remember that color is just the beginning—the successful look needs plenty of texture! These jackets will enhance your wardrobe with that most desirable quality. Choose a bouclé yarn to give Red Square the slubby/nubby appeal of designer textiles. Or create your own texture when you "chain" the front of Looped Loops. Café au Lait gives you visual texture by approaching stripes from two different sides, while Black & Bright surprises everyone with a panel of multicolor "lace." All are so eye-catching and so perfectly you!

LOOPED LOOPS

■■■□ INTERMEDIATE

TO FIT SIZES
- X-Small, Small, Medium, Large, X-Large
- Shown in size Medium.

FINISHED MEASUREMENTS
(Note that this is a boxy fit cardigan with extra ease at bust when worn with no closure.)
- Bust 38.5 (42, 46, 50, 54)"/ 98 (106.5, 117, 127, 137)cm
- Length
        23 (23, 23.5, 23.5, 24.5)"/ 58.5 (58.5, 59.5, 59.5, 62)cm

MATERIALS
Caron® Simply Soft® Paints
(each ball approx 4oz/113g, 100% acrylic, 200yds/182m)
- 4 (4, 4, 5, 5) balls in #8 Sunset (reds)
- 2 balls in #9 Sticks and Stones (browns)
- One each sizes I/5.5mm and J/6mm crochet hooks.

GAUGE
- 11 sts to 4"/10cm and 5 rows to 3"/7.5cm in double crochet using size J/6mm crochet hook.

- Main Color refers to the Reds or the body of the jacket.
- Contrast Color refers to the Browns, used at the lower edges and cuffs.
- Carry colors loosely along side edge until instructed to cut yarn.
- There are side vents at the lower edge of the jacket.
- Turn at the end of every row.

JACKET BACK

- With size J/6mm hook and Contrast Color, ch 53 (58, 64, 69, 74).

- Row 1 Work 1 dc in 4th ch from hook, then in each ch across = 51 (56, 62, 67, 72) dc.

- Row 2 (This row is the right side of the garment. When working in dc after each ch-12 loop, keep the loops in front of work.) Ch 3 for first dc, work 13 (13, 13, 15, 15) more dc, [ch 12, work 5 more dc] twice, ch 12, work remaining 27 (32, 38, 41, 46) dc across = 3 ch-12 loops will hang in front of work.

- Row 3 Ch 3 for first dc and work 1 dc in each dc across. Keep the ch-12 loops behind work.

- Row 4 Repeat row 2. Do not cut yarn.

- Rows 5 - 6 With Main Color, repeat rows 3 - 4. Do not cut yarn.

- Rows 7-16 In same way, continue to repeat rows 3 - 4, working 2 rows Contrast Color, then 2 rows Main Color, until you have 3 stripes each of Main Color and Contrast Color, with final stripe in Contrast Color. Cut Contrast Color and continue with Main Color only for rest of back.

- Repeat rows 3 - 4 with Main Color until piece measures 15.5"/39.5cm from beginning.

- Lengthen or shorten piece at this point by working more or less rows. It does not matter which row you end with.

- Cut yarn and fasten off.

SHAPE ARMHOLE

• Next row Skip first 4 (5, 7, 8, 9) sts, join yarn to next st and ch 3 for first dc, then continue pattern across to last 4 (5, 7, 8, 9) sts and leave them unworked for underarm.

• Continue in pattern as before AND decrease 1 st each side every right side row a total of 1 (2, 3, 4, 5) times.

• Continue in pattern as before, working on 41 (42, 42, 43, 44) sts, until armhole measures approx 7 (7, 7.5, 7.5, 8.5)"/18 (18, 19, 19, 21.5)cm, end having completed a right side row and ready to work the final dc row (a wrong side row).

• Loop the loops With the right side of work facing you, poke through the very first ch-12 loop at the lower edge and pull the 2nd loop (directly on top of it) through the first loop. In same way, pull the 3rd loop through the 2nd loop and so on up to the shoulder line. Let the final loop hang to the front. Do this for each of the next 2 columns of ch-12 loops.

"Style is an expression of individualism mixed with charisma. Fashion is something that comes after style."
– John Fairchild

• Final row With the wrong side of work facing you, work the final row of dc across the first 22 (25, 28, 29, 32) sts, [slip st into ch-12 loop to secure it, work 5 more dc] twice, secure last loop, work final 9 (7, 4, 4, 2) dc.

• Cut yarn and fasten off.

RIGHT FRONT

• With size J/6mm hook and Contrast Color, ch 28 (30, 33, 35, 39).

• Row 1 Work 1 row in dc as for back = 26 (28, 31, 33, 37) dc.

• Row 2 Ch 3 for first dc, work 2 (3, 2, 3, 5) more dc, [ch 12, work 5 more dc] 4 (4, 5, 5, 5) times, ch 12, work remaining 3 (4, 3, 4, 6) dc across = 5 (5, 6, 6, 6) ch-12 loops will hang in front of work.

• Work 6 rows more in pattern with Contrast Color, ending with a ch-12 row.

• Cut yarn and fasten off.

• With the loops facing you, begin with the first loop at lower left edge, and loop up to the 4th loop, leaving it hanging. Do the same for the 2nd row of loops from the left, leave the 3rd and 4th rows of loops as is, then loop up the final 1 (1, 2, 2, 2) rows of loops.

• With Main Color, work a wrong side row of dc and secure the looped loops as for the back.

• Complete piece with Main Color and continue the pattern as established on the remaining open ch-12 loops, until piece measures same as back to armhole.

SHAPE ARMHOLE

• Shape the armhole as for back by leaving 4 (5, 7, 8, 9) sts unworked at side edge (with the loop side of work facing you, this would be to your left) and then decreasing 1 st at the armhole edge every right side row 1 (2, 3, 4, 5) times.

SHAPE NECK

• When the armhole measures approx 3"/7.5cm less than back to shoulder, shape neck by leaving 7 (7, 7, 8, 9) sts unworked at neck edge (with the loop side of work facing you, this would be to your right) and then decreasing 1 st at neck edge every right side row twice.

• When the armhole measures same as back before the final wrong side row, loop the remaining 2 rows of loops to the shoulder, then work the final row and secure the loops as for the back.

• Cut yarn and fasten off.

LEFT FRONT

• This piece is worked by alternating 4 rows of Contrast Color with 4 rows of Main Color. Carry the yarns loosely up the side edges, cutting only when shaping armhole and neck (if necessary) and at end of final row.

- With size J/6mm hook and Contrast Color, ch 28 (30, 33, 35, 39). Work 1 row in dc as for right front.

- Row 2 Ch 3 for first dc, work 13 (13, 13, 15, 15) more dc, **[**ch 12, work 3 dc**]** twice, ch 12, work remaining 6 (8, 11, 11, 15) dc (this is center front edge).

- Continue in pattern as established, alternating 4 rows of each color, until piece measures same as right front to armhole.

SHAPE ARMHOLE AND NECK

- Shape the armhole as for back by leaving 4 (5, 7, 8, 9) sts unworked at side edge (with the loop side of work facing you, this would be to your right) and then decreasing 1 st at the armhole edge every right side row 1 (2, 3, 4, 5) times.

- Shape the neck as for right front by leaving 7 (7, 7, 8, 9) sts unworked at neck edge (with the loop side of work facing you, this would be to your right) and then decreasing 1 st at neck edge every right side row twice.

- When the armhole measures same as back before the final wrong side row, loop the 3 rows of loops to the shoulder, then work the final row and secure the loops as for the back.

- Cut yarn and fasten off.

SLEEVES

- Both sleeves have 8 rows of Contrast Color at cuff edge and are then finished with Main Color.

- With size J/6mm hook and Contrast Color, ch 27 (29, 29, 31, 31). Work 1 row in dc as for back.

- Row 2 Ch 3 for first dc, work 4 (5, 5, 6, 6) more dc, [ch 12, work 5 dc] 3 times, ch 12, work remaining 5 (6, 6, 7, 7) dc.

- Rows 3 - 8 Work 6 rows more in pattern. Cut yarn.

- Loop up the loops to final row. With Main Color, work a wrong side row of dc and secure each loop with a slip st.

- Continue with Main Color, working in rows of dc only, AND increase 1 st each side every 3rd row 5 times, then every 4th row twice. Work on 37 (37, 39, 41, 43) dc until piece is 18"/45.5cm from beginning, or desired length to underarm.

SHAPE CAP

- Leave 4 (5, 7, 8, 9) sts unworked at each edge and work 1 row dc on center 29 (27, 25, 25, 23) sts only.

- Work in dc and decrease 1 st each side every row 9 times.

- Work 1 row more and decrease 5 (5, 4, 4, 2) sts across the row.

- Work 1 row more in dc.

- Cut yarn and fasten off.

FINISHING

- Block pieces lightly.

- Sew each front to back at shoulder seams.

- Set in sleeves.

- Sew side and sleeve sleams, leaving 3 rows open at lower edge of body for side vents.

"Create your own visual style... let it be unique for yourself and yet identifiable for others."
— Orson Welles

FRONT AND NECK EDGING

• With right side facing and size I/5.5mm hook, join single strand of Main Color to lower edge of right front and ch 1, then work in sc evenly to top of neck edge. Hdc evenly around neck edge to Left Front, sc evenly across Left Front edge. Do not turn. Ch 2 and work 1 row of reverse single crochet.

• Cut yarn and fasten off.

• Weave in ends.

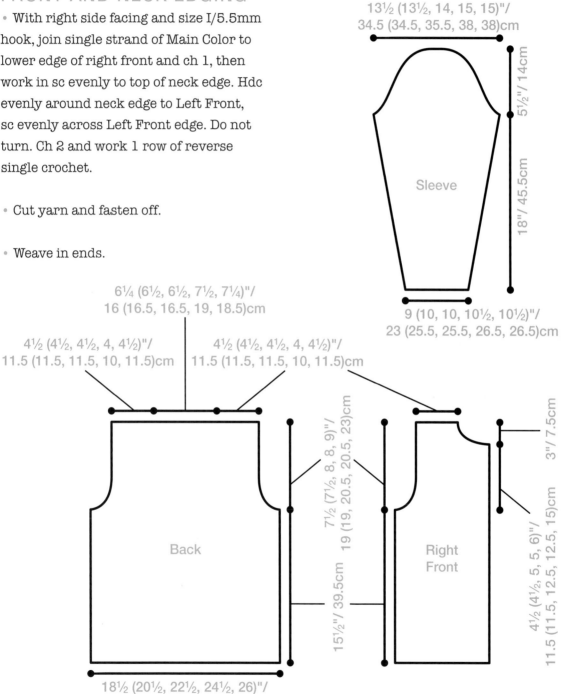

13½ (13½, 14, 15, 15)"/
34.5 (34.5, 35.5, 38, 38)cm

5½"/14cm

18"/45.5cm

Sleeve

9 (10, 10, 10½, 10½)"/
23 (25.5, 25.5, 26.5, 26.5)cm

6¼ (6½, 6½, 7½, 7¼)"/
16 (16.5, 16.5, 19, 18.5)cm

4½ (4½, 4½, 4, 4½)"/
11.5 (11.5, 11.5, 10, 11.5)cm

4½ (4½, 4½, 4, 4½)"/
11.5 (11.5, 11.5, 10, 11.5)cm

7½ (7½, 8, 8, 9)"/
19 (19, 20.5, 20.5, 23)cm

3"/7.5cm

Back

Right
Front

15½"/39.5cm

4½ (4½, 5, 5, 6)"/
11.5 (11.5, 12.5, 12.5, 15)cm

18½ (20½, 22½, 24½, 26)"/
47 (52, 57, 62, 66)cm

RED SQUARE

■■□□ **EASY +**

TO FIT SIZES

- X-Small, Small, Medium, Large, X-Large
- Shown in size Medium.

FINISHED MEASUREMENTS

(Note that there is at least an extra 2-3"/5-7.5cm worth of
ease at bust when worn with no closure.)

- Bust 33 (35.5, 38, 40, 43)"/
      84 (90, 96.5, 101.5, 109)cm
- Length (measured flat)
      20 (20.5, 21, 21.5, 21.5)"/
      51 (52, 53.5, 54.5, 54.5)cm

MATERIALS

Tahki Cotton Classic

(each skein approx 1.75oz/50g,
100% mercerized cotton, 108yds/100m)

- 8 (9, 9, 10, 10) skeins in #3997 Red

Tahki Punta

(each ball approx .9oz/25g, 100% nylon, 190yds/175m)

- 4 balls in #6 Fuchsia/Plum/Red
- One each sizes H/5mm and K/6.5mm crochet hooks.

GAUGE

- 13 sts and 7 rows to 4"/10cm in double crochet using
size K/6.5mm crochet hook and 1 strand of each yarn held
together.

NOTES

- Work the entire jacket with 1 strand of each yarn held together. Only the trim is worked with 1 strand of the solid color yarn.
- There are side vents at the lower edge of the jacket.
- Turn at the end of every row.

JACKET
BACK

- With size K/6.5mm hook and 1 strand of each yarn held together, ch 55 (59, 63, 67, 71).

- Row 1 Work 1 dc in 4th chain from hook, then in each chain across = 53 (57, 61, 65, 69) dc.

- Row 2 Ch 4 (counts as 1 dc and ch-1), *skip 1 dc, work 1 dc in next dc, ch 1; repeat from* across, end 1 dc in final dc = 27 (28, 30, 32, 34) ch-1 sps and 26 (29, 31, 33, 35) sc.

- Row 3 (This row is a right side row. Mark this side of piece as the right side of garment.) Ch 3 (counts as 1 dc), work 1 dc in each ch-1 sp and each dc across = 53 (57, 61, 65, 69) dc.

- Repeat rows 2-3 for pattern until piece measures 13"/33cm from beginning (stretch piece slightly to measure; a total of approx 21 rows), end with row 2.

- If you want to lengthen the piece, do so at this point by working a few more rows until desired length to underarm, making sure to end with row 2.

- Cut yarn and fasten off.

SHAPE ARMHOLE

- Next row Skip first 4 (4, 6, 7, 9) sts and sps, join yarn to next st or sp and ch 3 (counts as first dc), then work 44 (48, 48, 50, 50) more dc across, leaving last 4 (4, 6, 7, 9) sts for underarm.

- Continue in pattern as before (repeating rows 2-3), working on 45 (49, 49, 51, 51) sts, until armhole measures 7 (7.5, 8, 8.5, 8.5)"/18 (19, 20.5, 21.5, 21.5)cm, ending by working a right side row.

- Cut yarn and fasten off.

LEFT FRONT

- With size K/6.5mm hook and 1 strand of each yarn held together, ch 29 (31, 33, 35, 37).

- **Row 1** Work 1 dc in 4th ch from hook, then in each ch across = 27 (29, 31, 33, 35) dc.

- **Rows 2 - 3** Rep rows 2-3 as for back and work until piece measures same as back to armhole, end with row 2.

- Cut yarn and fasten off.

SHAPE ARMHOLE

- **Next Row** Skip first 4 (4, 6, 7, 9) sts and sps, join yarn to next st or sp and ch 3 (counts as first dc), then work 1 dc in each st and sp across = 23 (25, 25, 26, 26) dc.

- Continue in pattern as for back until piece measures same as back to shoulder.

SHAPE COLLAR

- Ch 3 and work 9 (10, 10, 12, 12) more dc.

- Turn and working ch 3 at beginning of every row, work 4 rows more in dc, AND increase 1 st at center front edge every row = 14 (15, 15, 17, 17) dc at end of final row.

- Cut yarn and fasten off.

RIGHT FRONT

- Work as for left front to armhole. Do not cut yarn at end of row 2 at armhole. Turn, ch 3 and work 22 (24, 24, 25, 25) more dc. Work as for left front to shoulder.

- Cut yarn and fasten off.

- Reverse collar shaping by joining yarn to center front, ch 3 and work 9 (10, 10, 12, 12) more dc. Work 4 rows more in dc and increase at center front edge as for left front.

- Cut yarn and fasten off.

SLEEVES

- With size K/6.5mm hook and 1 strand of each yarn held together, ch 37, (37, 37, 37, 39).

- **Row 1** Work 1 dc in 4th ch from hook, then in each ch across = 35 (35, 35, 35, 37) dc.

- **Rows 2 - 3** Rep rows 2-3 as for back, AND increase 1 st each side on 3rd row from beginning, then on 5th row and for sizes M, L and XL only, work a 3rd set of increases on 7th row from beginning = 39 (39, 41, 41, 43) dc. For all sizes, continue pattern until piece measures 6"/15cm from beginning, ending with row 2.

- Cut yarn and fasten off.

SHAPE CAP

• **Next Row** With right side of sleeve facing you, skip first 4 (4, 6, 7, 9) sts, join yarn to next st or sp and ch 3 (counts as first dc), then work 1 dc in next 30 (30, 28, 26, 24) sts and sps across, leaving final 4 (4, 6, 7, 9) sts open.

• Work same number of rows in pattern as for back from armhole to shoulder.

• Cut yarn and fasten off.

FINISHING

• Block pieces lightly.

• Sew each front to back at shoulder seams, sewing side edge of collar along back neck.

• Set in sleeves, matching rows on back and fronts to sleeve cap. Fold top of sleeve to center to form box pleat and tack to shoulder seam. Leave points free OR you can tack points at top of sleeve to jacket.

• Sew side and sleeve seams, leaving 3"/7.5cm open at lower edge of body for side vents.

PICOT EDGING

• With right side facing and size H/5mm hook, join single strand of solid color yarn to lower edge of sleeve at side seam and ch 1, work 2 sc along edge, *ch 3, then sc in first ch to form picot, work 3 sc evenly along edge; repeat from* around, end slip st to top of first ch-1 to join.

• Cut yarn and fasten off.

• Repeat for second sleeve.

• In same way, begin at lower edge of right front and work picot edging (working 5 sc in between picots) along right front and collar edge, back neck, opposite collar edge, then along left front to lower edge.

• Cut yarn and fasten off.

• Weave in ends.

When a solid won't do and a texture is too much (and too thin), get the best of both worlds and work with both yarns held together. "Runner" yarns (shown lower left) add texture and interest with little effect on gauge and certainly no effort on your part.

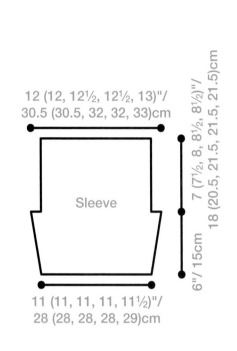

12 (12, 12½, 12½, 13)"/
30.5 (30.5, 32, 32, 33)cm

Sleeve

7 (7½, 8, 8½, 8½)"/
18 (20.5, 21.5, 21.5, 21.5)cm

6"/ 15cm

11 (11, 11, 11, 11½)"/
28 (28, 28, 28, 29)cm

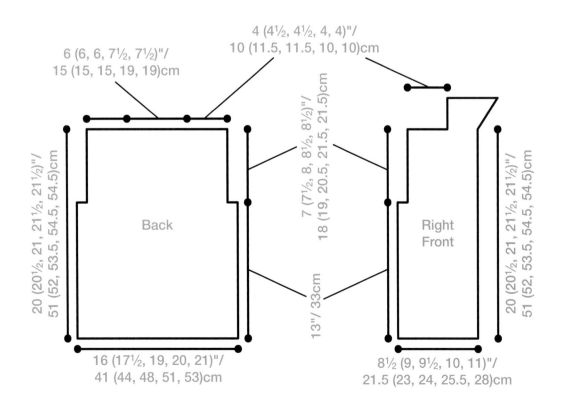

6 (6, 6, 7½, 7½)"/
15 (15, 15, 19, 19)cm

4 (4½, 4½, 4, 4)"/
10 (11.5, 11.5, 10, 10)cm

Back

20 (20½, 21, 21½, 21½)"/
51 (52, 53.5, 54.5, 54.5)cm

7 (7½, 8, 8½, 8½)"/
18 (19, 20.5, 21.5, 21.5)cm

13"/ 33cm

Right Front

20 (20½, 21, 21½, 21½)"/
51 (52, 53.5, 54.5, 54.5)cm

16 (17½, 19, 20, 21)"/
41 (44, 48, 51, 53)cm

8½ (9, 9½, 10, 11)"/
21.5 (23, 24, 25.5, 28)cm

CAFÉ AU LAIT

◼◼◻◻ **EASY +**

SIZE

• Our model is wearing the sample size (see measurements below). She is 5'11"/180cm tall with a 34"/86.5cm bust.
• See the schematic on page 23 and see page 27 for instructions on customizing bust and length.

FINISHED MEASUREMENTS

• Bust 68"/172.5cm
• Length 27"/68.5cm

MATERIALS

Red Heart® Super Saver®

(Solids: each skein approx 7oz/198g, 100% acrylic, 364yds/333m)
• 2 skeins each in following colors:
    #0360 Cafe
    #0334 Buff
    #0336 Warm Brown

(Prints/multis: each skein approx 5oz/141g, 100% acrylic, 244yds/223m)
• 2 skeins each in following colors:
    #0792 Sandy Print
    #0992 Shaded Browns

(Flecks: each skein approx 5oz/141g, 96% acrylic, 4% other fibers, 260yds/238m)
• 2 skeins each in following colors:
    #4334 Buff Fleck
    #4313 Aran Fleck
• One each sizes I/5.5mm and K/6.5mm crochet hooks.

GAUGE

• 11 sts and 7 rows to 4"/10cm in double crochet using size K/6.5mm crochet hook.

NOTES

The colors are used in this order for the stripe pattern for both the right and left halves:

- A. Warm Brown (solid)
- B. Sandy Print (print)
- C. Buff (solid)
- D. Shaded Browns (print)
- E. Cafe (solid)
- F. Buff Fleck (solid w/flecks
- G. Aran Fleck (solid w/flecks)

Repeat rows A - G for color stripe pattern.

TOPPER
LEFT HALF

Please read through notes on page 27 before beginning this.

- With size K/6.5mm hook and A, ch 26, ch 1 (mark this for corner), ch 6 (underarm), ch 1 (mark this for corner), ch 26, then ch 2 for the turning ch = a total of 62 chs.

- Row 1 With A, work 1 dc in 4th ch from hook, then in each of 25 chs, work 2 dc in marked st (corner), work 1 dc in each of next 6 chs, work 2 dc in marked st (corner), work 1 dc in each of next 26 chs. Mark this row as right side of work.

- Cut yarn and fasten off.

• Row 2 With right side facing, join B to top of turning chain of row 1 and ch 2, then work 1 dc in each of next 26 dc, work 4 dc in between the 2-dc corner of previous row, work 1 dc in each of next 8 dc, work 4 dc in 2-dc corner as before, work 1 dc in each of next 27 dc.

• Cut yarn and fasten off.

• Rows 3 - 10 With RS facing, join next color and ch 2, work dc to corner, work 4 dc in between the center sts of 4-dc corner of previous row, dc to next corner, work 4 dc in corner as before, dc across.

• Row 11 With right side facing, join next color and ch 2, work 1 dc in each dc until 1 st before corner, work 2 dc in that st, work 2 dc in corner (in between the sts below as before), dc to next corner, work 2 dc in corner, then work 2 dc in st immediately following, then 1 dc in each st across to end.

• Rows 12 - 23 Repeat row 11.

• Row 24 With right side facing, join next color and ch 2, work pattern to last 7 sts of row (this is neck edge), work 1 hdc in next st.

• Cut yarn and fasten off.

• Rows 25 - 28 Work pattern to last 3 sts of row, work 2dc-tog (decrease at neck edge), work last st.

• Cut yarn and fasten off.

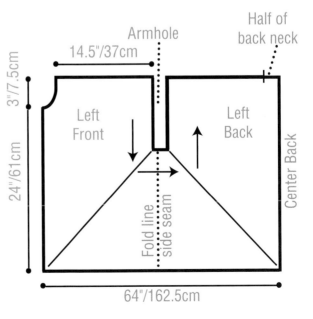

23

TOPPER
RIGHT HALF

- With size K/6.5mm hook and A, ch 26, ch 1 and mark this for corner, ch 6 (underarm), ch 1 and mark this for corner, ch 26, then ch 2 for the turning ch = a total of 62 chs.

- Row 1 With A, work as for row 1 of left half. Do not cut yarn. Turn.

- Row 2 With A, ch 2 (turning ch), then work 1 dc in each of next 26 dc, work 4 dc in between the 2-dc corner of previous row, work 1 dc in each of next 8 dc, work 4 dc in 2-dc corner as before, work 1 dc in each of next 27 dc.

- Cut yarn and fasten off. Turn.

"Style is the dress of thoughts."
— Lord Chesterfield

- Row 3 Work same as Left Half, do not cut yarn. Turn.

- Row 4 Ch 2, work dc to corner, work 4 dc in between the center sts of 4-dc corner of previous row, dc to next corner, work 4 dc in corner as before, dc across.

- Rows 5 - 10 Rep rows 3-4, continuing color sequence. You're working 1 dc in each dc to corner and working 4 dc in each corner.

- Row 11 With right side facing, join F and ch 2, work 1 dc in each dc until 1 st before corner, work 2 dc in that st, work 2 dc in corner (in between the sts in corner below), dc to next corner, work 2 dc in corner, then work 2 dc in st immediately following, then 1 dc in each st across to end. Turn.

- Row 12 Ch 2, work 1 dc in each dc until 1 st before corner, work 2 dc in that st, work 2 dc in corner (in between the sts below as before), dc to next corner, work 2 dc in corner, then work 2 dc in st immediately following, then 1 dc in each st across to end.

- Rows 13 - 23 Repeat rows 11-12, working G, then A through E.

• Row 24 With E, slip st through first 7 sts (this is neck edge), 1 hdc in next st, finish row in pattern.

• Rows 25 - 28 Continue pattern and work 2dc-tog (decrease) at neck edge.

• Cut yarn and fasten off.

• Block each piece lightly.

• Fold each piece in half (use schematic as guide) and sew or crochet shoulder seams, matching stripes and leaving neck open.

• Sew center back seam, leaving approx 4"/10cm at lower edge open for back vent.

SLEEVE EDGINGS (WORKED IN ROUNDS)

• Rnd 1 With right side of garment facing you and size K/6.5mm hook, join A to middle of underarm, ch 3 and FPdc around next 5 dc, 2 FPdc tog, (FPdc around next 5 dc, 2 FPdc tog) 7 times, FPdc around each dc to end. Join with slip st to first ch-3.

You can clearly see the single row stripes on the left back and the double row stripes on the right back.

- Rnd 2 Ch 3 and FPdc around each st to end. Join with slip st to first ch-3.

- Rnd 3 With size I/5.5mm hook, ch 2, work reverse single crochet in each st around. End slip st to first ch-2.

- Cut yarn and fasten off.

COLLAR

- Row 1 With right side of garment facing you and size I/5.5mm hook, join A to right front neck edge. Ch 2, work in sc evenly across to left front neck edge. Turn.

- Rows 2 - 6 Ch 2 at beginning of every row and work as follows: 1 row sc, then 4 rows hdc.

- Rows 7 - 10 Change to size K/6.5mm hook and work 4 rows in dc.

- Cut yarn and fasten off.

COLLAR EDGING

- With size I/5.5mm hook and right side of collar facing you, join A to left front neck edge and work sc evenly around, working 3 sc in each corner. Do not turn. Ch 2, work 1 row in reverse single crochet.

- Cut yarn and fasten off.

FINAL BORDER

- With right side of garment facing and size I/5.5mm hook, join C to left front neck edge. Ch 2 and work 1 row sc evenly around piece to center of back vent. Pause, try on and decide if you need to adjust fullness of piece. Re-do if necessary. Do not turn. Ch 2 and work 1 row reverse sc.

- In same way, work border around right half, beginning at center of back vent (see photo on page 25.)

- Cut yarn and fasten off.

- Weave in ends.

- Block entire piece.
Yesssssssssss - you did it!

CUSTOMIZE

CUSTOM SIZE

• Begin piece and work through several rows to familiarize yourself with construction.

• Continue to work in pattern until your piece is approximately 10"/25.5cm from underarm.

• Fold piece in half and baste shoulders.

• Try on and decide about width. Keep in mind that this garment is meant to be a topper, worn as an outside layer. Try it on over turtlenecks or jackets to get an idea of the most comfortable fit for you.

• Because of the construction, when you widen the piece, you will also lengthen it.

• Continue to work in pattern until shoulder is approx 2.5"/6.5cm less than your desired width.

• Shape the neckline and finish piece.

• Use the final finishing border around the entire edge to bring in extra fullness.

LEFT FRONT AND BACK

• Worked in one piece starting at armhole.

• Arrows on schematic, page 23, indicate direction of work.

• Work 1 row of each color, starting with A and working through G.

• Do not turn at end of every row. Begin each row with the right side of garment facing you.

• Cut yarn at end of each row, leaving approx a 3"/7.5cm tail. When possible, crochet over yarn tails at beginning and end of rows.

• Continue to mark the corners until you become familiar with their placement.

RIGHT FRONT AND BACK

• Work 2 rows of each color, starting with A and working through G.

• Turn at end of every row.

• Cut yarn at end of every other row, leaving approx a 3"/7.5cm tail. When possible, crochet over the yarn tails.

• Continue to mark the corners until you become familiar with their placement.

BLACK 'N BRIGHT

■■■□ INTERMEDIATE

TO FIT SIZES

Small (Medium, Large)

Our model is wearing size large. She is 5'11"/180cm tall with a 34"/86.5cm bust measurement.

FINISHED MEASUREMENTS

Bust 48 (56, 64)"/122 (142, 162.5)cm

Length 25"/63.5cm

Piece is measured flat, not including side fretwork.

MATERIALS

Red Heart® Super Saver®

(Solids: each skein approx 7oz/198g, 100% acrylic, 364yds/333m)

• 3 skeins in #0312 Black

(Prints/multis: each skein approx 5oz/141g, 100% acrylic, 244yds/223m)

• 2 skeins in #0723 Pinata

• One each sizes J/6mm and K/6.5mm crochet hooks.

GAUGE

• 11 sts and 7 rows to 4"/10cm in double crochet using size K/6.5mm crochet hook.

BACK
FOR ALL SIZES

- With size K/6.5mm hook and Main Color, ch 68 plus 2 extra for turning ch. (See note on page 33 on how to shorten piece.)

- Row 1 Work 1 sc in 3rd ch from hook, then in each ch across = 68 sc.

- Cut yarn and fasten off. Do not turn work.

- Row 2 Starting at beginning of row 1, join Contrast Color, ch 2 for turning ch and work 1 hdc in each sc across.

- Cut yarn and fasten off. Do not turn.

- Row 3 Starting at beginning of row 2, join Main Color, ch 3 for turning ch and working in back loops only, work 1 dc in each st across. Ch 3, turn.

FOR SIZE SMALL ONLY

- Rows 4-6 Work 3 rows more in dc working in both loops.

- Cut yarn and fasten off.

- Repeat rows 2 - 6, 7 times, then repeat row 2 once more = 9 stripes of Contrast Color.

FOR SIZE MEDIUM ONLY

- Rows 4-7 Work 4 rows more in dc working in both loops.

- Cut yarn and fasten off.

- Repeat rows 2 - 7, 7 times, then repeat row 2 once more = 9 stripes of Contrast Color.

FOR SIZE LARGE ONLY

- Rows 4-8 Work 5 rows more in dc working in both loops.

- Cut yarn and fasten off.

- Repeat rows 2 - 8, 7 times, then repeat row 2 once more = 9 stripes of Contrast Color.

FOR ALL SIZES

- Final row Starting at beginning of last Contrast Color row, join Main Color, ch 2 for turning ch and work sc in back loop only of each hdc across.

- Cut yarn and fasten off.

LEFT & RIGHT FRONTS

- Work as for back, repeating correct number of rows for your size in Main Color 3 times, then repeat row 2 once more = 5 stripes of Contrast Color. Work final row.

FINISHING
(The same finishing applies to all sizes.)

- Decide which side you want to be the right side of the garment. Place a marker on this side on all pieces so there is no confusion.

Braid At Lower Edge Of Back:

• Row 1 With right side of garment facing you, join Main Color to one corner, *ch 3, sc into edge; repeat from* evenly across. Use the rows of hdc and dc as a guide; I worked the sc into every row of hdc and dc.

• Cut yarn and fasten off.

• Row 2 With right side of garment facing you, join Contrast Color to first ch-3 sp, *ch 3, remove loop from hook, then insert hook from front to back through next ch-3 sp and pull the loop through the sp; repeat from* across.

• Cut yarn and fasten off.

• Repeat this braid edging along lower edges of both the left and right fronts.

SHOULDER EDGE

• On the back, mark the center 7"/18cm for the neck.

• Using schematic and stripes as guide, sew or crochet shoulder seams together, leaving marked back neck open and approx 3.5"/9cm at center of each front open - 4 stripes (counting from the side edge) will be joined together on each shoulder. Work fretwork (below).

FRETWORK AT SIDE EDGES

• Place a marker approx 3"/7.5cm from lower edge on either side of back ("A" on schematic).

• Place a 2nd marker approx 10"/25.5cm down from shoulders on either side of back ("B" on schematic).

• Do the same on the side edges of left and right fronts.

• Row 1 With the right side of garment facing you and size K/6.5mm hook, join Contrast Color to first marker at lower edge of back, *ch 3, skip 1 st and sc into next st; rep from* to 2nd marker = approx 17 ch-3 spaces; a few more or less is not critical. Turn.

- Row 2 Ch 3, sc into first ch-3 sp, *ch 3, sc in next ch-3 sp; repeat from* across. Turn.

- Rows 3 - 4 Repeat row 2.

- Row 5 Join back to right front as follows: Ch 1, sc in right front at first marker (A), ch 1, sc in first ch-3 sp, *ch 1, skip 1 st on right front and sc in next st, ch 1, sc in next ch-3 sp; repeat from* across to 2nd marker (B), ending with ch 1, sc in final ch-3 sp, ch 1, sc to right front.

- Cut yarn and fasten off.

- Work fretwork along opposite side as follows: Begin the fretwork at lower edge of left front, work rows 1-4, then connect to back when working row 5.

COLLAR

- With size J/6mm hook and right side of garment facing you, join Main Color to corner of right front, ch 2 and work 1 row of sc evenly around neck edge to corner of left front. Pull in the back neck slightly by working fewer sc across that space.

- Cut yarn and fasten off. Do not turn. Complete collar with Contrast Color.

- Row 1 With size J/6mm hook, join Contrast Color to edge of right front, ch 2 and work in hdc. Turn.

- Rows 2 - 4 Ch 2, work 1 hdc in each st across.

- Rows 5 - 6 Change to size K/6.5mm hook and work 2 rows more.

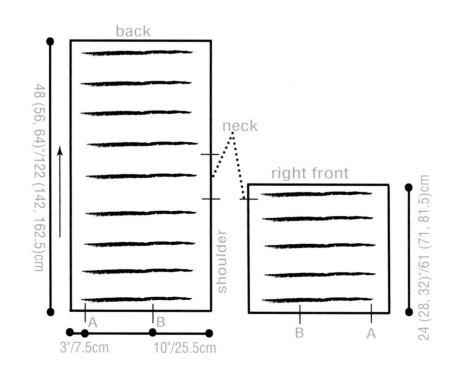

- Rows 7 and 9 Work across and increase 1 st at beginning, middle and end of row.

- Rows 8, 10 and 11 Work across in hdc.

- Cut yarn and fasten off.

- With size J/6mm hook and right side of collar facing, join yarn to left front neck edge, ch 2 and work 1 row sc evenly across entire collar to right front neck edge, working 3 sc in each corner. Do not turn.

- Ch 2, work 1 row reverse single crochet evenly across.

- Cut yarn and fasten off.

OPTIONAL: EDGE ARMHOLES

- With size J/6mm hook and right side of garment facing you, join Main Color to lower side of armhole and work 1 row reverse single crochet, decreasing 1 st each side of shoulder seam and leaving fretwork unworked.

- Cut yarn and fasten off.

- Weave in ends.

- Block entire piece lightly.

"Style is a simple way of saying complicated things."
– Jean Cocteau

CUSTOMIZE

- To shorten the length, chain 3 sts less for each 1"/2.5cm. For example, for a length of 24"/61cm, chain 65 plus 2 extra.
- For a length of 23"/58.5cm, you would chain 62 plus 2 extra. Remember to do the same for each front.
- The back, left and right fronts begin at the side edge.
- The arrow indicates direction of work.

SKIRTS & TOPS

When it comes to skirts, we live in an age when hemlines are anyone's call—calf, knee, mid-thigh, or higher! To get the right length for you, the two skirt patterns tell you how to allow for the natural relaxation of yarn fibers after they're washed. Both skirts are worked circularly from the waist, with the crochet hooks increasing in size as you go. Top off your separates with an Aqua Geo pullover and its fun variation, Geo Tan. Feel free to customize! The fun is about to begin....

AQUA GEO

EASY

TO FIT SIZES

X-Small, Small, Medium, Large, X-Large
Our model is wearing size Small.

FINISHED MEASUREMENTS

- Bust 36 (40, 44, 48, 52)"/91.5 (101.5, 112, 122, 132)cm
- Length 18 (20, 22, 24, 26)"/45.5 (51, 56, 61, 66)cm
      (Piece is measured flat.)

MATERIALS

Tahki Cotton Classic

(each skein approx 1.75oz/50g, 100% mercerized cotton,
108yds/100m)

- Main Color: 7 (8, 8, 10, 10) skeins in #3772 Bright Aqua
- Contrast Color: 1 skein in #3001 White
- Size I/5mm crochet hook.

GAUGE

- 16 sts and 8 rows to 4"/10cm in treble crochet using size
I/5mm crochet hook.

*"Fashion is architecture;
it is a matter of proportions."
– Coco Chanel*

GAME PLAN

Begin at the center by making the circular motif (rounds 1-3).

Work 4 more rounds to form a square from the circle (rounds 4-7).

Repeat round 7 to enlarge and size the square.

Add the neck edge along the top of front and back.

Put armholes and side edges together.

Work the lower edge to complete a rectangular pullover with a boat neck.

SPECIAL STITCH

5-dctog (uses one space)

• Yarn over, insert hook into space and pull up a loop, yarn over and pull through 2 loops; rep from* 3 times more, yarn over and pull through all 5 loops on hook.

PULLOVER
BACK AND FRONT

Make 2 pieces exactly the same.

• With size I/5mm hook and Main Color, ch 7, then join with a slip st to form a ring.

• Rnd 1 Ch 2, then work 19 dc in ring, end slip st to top of first ch-2.

• Rnd 2 Ch 4, [dc in next dc, ch 2] 19 times, end slip st to 3rd ch of first ch-4 = 20 ch-2 sps around.

• Rnd 3 Ch 2, *work 5-dctog in next sp, ch 3; rep from* around, end slip st to top of first 5-dctog.

• Rnd 4 Ch 2 (counts as 1 sc), work 2 sc in ch-3 sp, *3 dc in next ch-3 sp, work (3 tr, ch 3, 3 tr) in next ch-3 sp (this is a corner), 3 dc in next ch-3 sp, 3 sc in each of next 2 ch-3 sps; rep from* around, end 3 sc in final ch-3 sp, then slip st to top of first ch-2 = 4 corners made.

• Rnd 5 *Ch 3, (hdc in dc) 3 times, (dc in tr) 3 times, work (3 dc, ch 3, 3 dc) in ch-3 sp for corner, (dc in tr) 3 times, (hdc in dc) 3 times, ch 3, sc between 3rd and 4th sc; rep from* around, end with ch 1, dc between 3rd and 4th sc (this is final ch-3 sp).

- Rnd 6 Sc in same ch-3 sp just made, ch 5, sc in next ch-3 space, *ch 5, skip 3 hdcs, (dc in dc) 6 times, work (3 dc, ch 3, 3 dc) in corner ch-3 sp, (dc in dc) 6 times, sk 3 hdc, (ch 5, sc in next ch-3 sp) twice; rep from* around, end ch 2, dc in first sc (this is final ch-5 sp).

- Rnd 7 Sc in same ch-5 sp just made, *(ch 5, sc in next ch-5 sp) twice, ch 5, skip 3 dc, (dc in dc) 6 times, work (3 dc, ch 3, 3 dc) in corner ch-3 sp, (dc in dc) 6 times, ch 5, sc in next ch-5 sp; rep from* around, end ch 2, dc in first sc (this is final ch 5).

- Continue to repeat rnd 7, working one more ch-5 between each corner, until piece, slightly stretched, measures approx 16 (18, 20, 22, 24)"/40.5 (45.5, 51, 56, 61)cm across a straight edge, ending with ch 2, dc in first sc to complete a rnd.

- Final rnd Ch 2 (counts as 1 hdc), 1 hdc in same space, work 4 hdc in each ch-5 space around, work 5 hdc in each corner ch-3 space and work 1 hdc in each dc around. Work 2 hdc in final ch-5 space, then slip st to first ch-2.

- Cut yarn and fasten off.

- Block both pieces lightly.

BORDER AT TOP EDGE

(This is the neck edge; work border on both front and back.)

- Row 1 With right side of piece facing you and Main Color, join yarn to any corner hdc, ch 2, then work 1 row sc across to next corner.

- Cut yarn and fasten off.

- Row 2 With right side still facing you and Contrast Color, join yarn to first st on row 1, then ch 2 and work 1 row sc across, working in back loops only of Main Color.

- Cut yarn and fasten off.

- Row 3 With right side still facing you and Main Color, join yarn to first st on row 2, then ch 2 and work 1 row sc across, working in back loops only of Contrast Color.

- Cut yarn and fasten off.

SIDE EDGES

(Work side edges on both front and back.)

- With right side of piece facing you, join Main Color to corner of piece at neck edge, ch 2 and work 1 row sc along side edge.

- Work 1 row of sc along opposite side edge, joining at bottom corner.

- Cut yarn and fasten off.

FINISHING

Join shoulders and side edges

• Mark the center 8.5 (8.5, 9.5, 9.5, 9.5)"/21.5 (21.5, 24, 24, 24)cm at center of top edge (where the Contrast Color stripe is) for neck opening.

• With wrong sides of back and front together and right side of pieces facing you, use Main Color and single crochet shoulders together, working through both pieces and leaving center marked space open.

*"Style is the perfection of a point of view."
— Richard Eberhart*

• Mark 6.5 (6.5, 7, 7, 7.5)"/16.5 (16.5, 18, 18, 19)cm down from shoulders on front and back for armhole. With the right side of garment facing you and Main Color, single crochet side edges together through both thicknesses, from lower edge to armhole opening.

NECK EDGING

• With the right side of garment facing you, join Contrast Color to neck edge, ch 2 and work 1 rnd in sc, working in back loops only.

• Cut yarn and fasten off. Do not turn.

• Join Main Color and work 1 round reverse single crochet.

• Cut yarn and fasten off.

40

ARMHOLE EDGING

• Rnd 1 With the right side of garment facing you, join Contrast Color to armhole edge, ch 2 and work 1 rnd hdc, working in back loops only and end with slip st to join.

• Cut yarn and fasten off. Do not turn.

• Rnd 2 Join Main Color and work 1 rnd reverse single crochet, AND decrease 1 st each side of shoulder seam (working sc2tog) to curve top of armhole.

• Cut yarn and fasten off.

LOWER EDGE

• With RS facing, join MC to lower edge and work approx 1"/2.5cm in sc evenly around, working in back loops only. Join with slip st to first sc.

• Do not turn. Ch 2, then work 1 round reverse single crochet.

• Cut yarn and fasten off.

• Weave in ends.

• Block entire pullover, carefully smoothing out any kinks in the central motif.

The fretwork that you see filling in the crossed "X" tends to pull in, thus giving the pullover a natural shape around the waistline. Take this into consideration when blocking. By concentrating on the quadrants near the face and lower edge, you can coax the pieces into a rectangle with the side edges curving in a bit.

GEO TAN

EASY

FINISHED MEASUREMENTS

(Piece is measured flat.)

- Bust 52"/132cm
- Length 27"/68.5cm

MATERIALS

TLC® Cotton Plus™

(each ball approx 3.5oz/100g, 51% cotton, 49% acrylic, 178yds/163m)

- 6 balls in #3303 Tan
- Optional: approx 30yds/27.5m of novelty yarn.
- Size K/6.5mm crochet hook.

GAUGE

- 16 sts and 8 rows to 4"/10cm in treble crochet using size K/6.5mm crochet hook.

*"If you always do what interests you,
at least one person is pleased."
– Katherine Hepburn*

GAME PLAN

Starting at the center, work rounds 1-3 as for Aqua Geo pullover. Optional: Use a textured yarn for round 3.

Work rounds 4-7 as for pullover to form a square.

Repeat round 7 to form the large "X." Optional: Use a textured yarn as desired on the 3rd repeat of round 7 to form a textured square around the central circle.

Work edgings at top of front and back. Finish neckline.

Work side edges. You can make the piece wider by working more rows. Finish armholes.

Work hem at lower edge to desired length. After you've worn the piece, it will stretch. You can easily add or subtract a few rows as desired.

PULLOVER
BACK AND FRONT

• Follow the instructions for the Aqua Geo pullover (pp 38-39), using the game plan at left as a guide.

• Repeat rnd 7 until piece measures 24"/61cm across, measuring piece slightly stretched.

• Work the final rnd.

• Block both front and back.

• Before working the top and side edges, baste the 2 pieces together and try on. This will give you an idea of how much larger and longer you want the piece to be. OR you may want it smaller and shorter, and you can easily take out a few rounds at this point. Don't worry about the shoulder line sticking out. This is resolved in the finishing. Hang the basted pieces from a coat hanger overnight AND/OR wash and dry the 2 pieces to allow for all possible stretch.

BORDER AT TOP EDGE

• With right side of piece facing you and Main Color, join yarn to any corner hdc, ch 2, then work 1 row sc across to next corner in back loops only.

• Cut yarn and fasten off.

• Row 2 Copy from Aqua Geo.

- Row 3 With right side still facing you and Main Color, join yarn to first st on Row 2, then ch 2 and work 1 row sc across, working in both loops of Contrast Color.

- Cut yarn and fasten off.

SIDE EDGES

- Row 1 With right side of piece facing you, join Main Color in corner of piece at neck edge, ch 2 and work sc along edge. Turn.

- Row 2 and 4 Ch 1, work 1 sc in front loop only of each st across. Turn.

- Row 3 Ch 1, work 1 sc in back loop only of each st across. Turn.

- Cut yarn and fasten off.

FINISHING

Follow the finishing instructions on page 40 following instructions for largest size.

NECK EDGING AND ARMHOLE EDGING

- Work same as Aqua Geo, pages 40-41, using Main Color, do not fasten off after Rnd 1.

LOWER EDGE

- With right side facing, join Main Color to lower edge and work 1 rnd sc. Join with slip st to first sc.

- Do not turn. Ch 2, then work 1 rnd reverse single crochet.

- Cut yarn and fasten off.

- Weave in ends.

- Block entire pullover, carefully smoothing out any kinks in the central motif.

To create an A-line shape on the tunic or pullover, make the front and back, including shoulder and neck. Measure and mark for the armhole. Work one side edge beginning at the shoulder line and when you are an inch or so below the armhole, switch to half double crochet for another few inches; then double crochet until you reach the lower edge. Work as many rows as necessary. Work the other 3 side edges to match.

KING TUT

 EASY

TO FIT SIZES
- X-Small, Small, Medium, Large, X-Large
- Shown in size Medium.

FINISHED MEASUREMENTS
- Waist 30 (32.5, 35, 37.5, 40)"/ 76 (82.5, 89, 95.5, 101.5)cm
- Length approx 27"/68.5cm

(you may need extra yarn if you plan to make this longer)

MATERIALS

Berroco® Pure® Merino DK

(each skein approx 1.75oz/50g, 100% extra fine merino, 126yds/115m)
- 8 (9, 9, 10, 10) skeins in #4576 Coal Tar
- One each sizes H/5mm, I/5.5mm, J/6mm and K/6.5mm crochet hooks.

GAUGE
- 13 sts and 10 rows to 4"/10cm in pattern using size H/5mm crochet hook.

Making skirts without side seams helps eliminate assorted bags and sags. As there is no back or front, you can wear the skirt any which way every day and thus not place regular stress on any particular area.

NOTES

• Skirt is worked circularly in one piece, beginning at the waist and ending at the hemline.

• The skirt is designed to have a very slender fit with little to no ease allowed with increased stitches. The increase in size from waist to hem is determined by using progressively larger crochet hooks. Increases are done only to form the ruffle at lower edge.

• After joining with slip st at end of each rnd and working beginning ch of next rnd, turn your work so you are working in the opposite direction. Each rnd is worked in this manner.

SKIRT

• With size H/5mm hook, ch 100 (108, 116, 124, 132).

• Row 1 Work 1 dc in 4th chain from hook, then in each chain across = 98 (106, 114, 122, 130) dc. Being careful not to twist this first row of sts, join with a slip st to form a ring. It doesn't matter which side is facing when you join. Just make sure that if you were to fold the ring flat and in half, it does not have a twist in the middle of it. Turn.

• Rnd 1 Ch 3, then work 1 dc in between each st around, end slip st to top of first ch-3.

• Rnd 2 Ch 3, turn your work and going in the opposite direction, work 1 dc in between each st around, end slip st to top of first ch-3.

• Rnd 3 Ch 3, turn your work and going in the opposite direction (the same direction as in rnd 1), work 1 dc in between each st around, end slip st to top of first ch-3.

• Repeat rnds 2 - 3, remembering to turn and work each rnd in the opposite direction of the previous rnd, until piece measures approx 4.5"/11.5cm from beginning, slightly stretched.

• Change to size I/5.5mm hook.

• Repeat rnds 2-3 as before, cont to turn work at beginning of each rnd, until piece measures approx 9"/23cm from beginning.

Try skirt on so you can see how it suits your body. Because you are using pure wool, bear in mind that you can block approx 1"/2.5cm worth of ease into the fabric.

• Change to size J/6mm hook.

• Repeat rnds 2 - 3, working 1 dc in between each dc around, until piece measures approx 4"/10cm less than desired finished length.

Let the skirt hang out for a day or so and/ or wash/dry the skirt.

Try on skirt and decide on final length. Since you want to end approx 4"/10cm before your final desired length, rip back or work as many rnds as necessary.

• Change to size K/6.5mm hook.

• Work 2"/5cm more rnds of dc as before, working in between sts of previous rnd.

RUFFLE

• Rnd 1 (increase rnd) *Work 1 dc in between 2 dc, then work 2 dc in between next 2 dc; repeat from* around, end slip st to top of first ch-3. It's all right if you don't have enough sts to complete the repeat. Just work 1 extra single dc between 2 dc to get to the end of the rnd.

• Rnd 2 Ch 3, turn your work and work 1 dc in between each dc around, end slip st to top of first ch-3.

• Rnd 3 (increase rnd) Repeat rnd 1.

• Rnd 4 - 5 Repeat rnd 2.

• Final rnd (increase rnd) Repeat rnd 1.

• Cut yarn and fasten off.

• Weave in ends. Sew first row closed at beginning of skirt.

MAKE DRAWSTRING

• With size I/5.5mm hook, chain a length that will fit comfortably around your waist with enough extra to tie into a small bow. Tie around your waist and lengthen or shorten as necessary.

• Turn and work 1 slip st in each chain to the end.

• Cut yarn and fasten off.

• Weave in ends. Weave drawstring through top of skirt and adjust to fit.

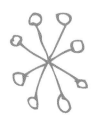

USING ELASTIC

Cut a length of 1"/2.5cm elastic in appropriate color to fit evenly around your waist, with approximately 1"/2.5cm extra at each end. Bear in mind that it must stretch to fit around your hips as you step into the skirt, or around your shoulders and bust if you intend to pull the skirt over your head. Overlap the ends together and sew securely.

Pin the elastic evenly to skirt. Using herringbone stitch, sew elastic into position.

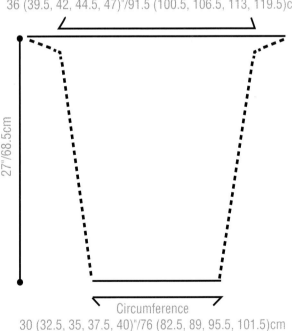

Circumference
36 (39.5, 42, 44.5, 47)"/91.5 (100.5, 106.5, 113, 119.5)cm

27"/68.5cm

Circumference
30 (32.5, 35, 37.5, 40)"/76 (82.5, 89, 95.5, 101.5)cm

TWEEDY PIE

◨■□□ **EASY**

TO FIT SIZES

- X-Small, Small, Medium, Large, X-Large
- Shown in size X-Small.

FINISHED MEASUREMENTS

- Waist 30.5 (32, 34, 36, 38)"/ 77.5 (81.5, 86.5, 91.5, 96.5)cm
- Length approx 21"/53.5cm

(you may need extra yarn if you plan to make this longer)

MATERIALS

Caron® Simply Soft® Shadows

(each skein approx 3oz/85g, 100% acrylic, 150yds/137m)
- 4 (5, 5, 6, 6) skeins in #8 Opal Twist
- One each sizes J/6mm, K/6.5mm, L/8mm and M/9mm
crochet hooks.

GAUGE

- 12 sts and 10 rows to 4"/10cm in half double crochet using
size J/6mm crochet hook.

A drawstring allows you to adjust the waistline a little lower some days, a little higher on others. Consider using narrow ribbon or rayon cording to weave through the waist.

NOTES

- Skirt is worked circularly in one piece, beginning at the waist and ending at the hemline.
- The increase in size from waist to hem is determined by using progressively larger crochet hooks as well as increased stitches.
- After joining with slip st at end of each rnd and working beginning ch of next rnd, turn your work so you are working in the opposite direction. Each rnd is worked in this manner.

SKIRT

- With size J/6mm hook, ch 94 (98, 104, 110, 116).

- Row 1 Work 1 hdc in 4th chain from hook, then in each chain across = 92 (96, 102, 108, 114) hdc. Being careful not to twist this first row of sts, join with a slip st to form a ring. It doesn't matter which side is facing when you join. Just make sure that if you were to fold the ring flat and in half, it does not have a twist in the middle of it. Turn.

- Rnd 1 Ch 2, then work 1 hdc in each st around, end slip st to top of first ch-2.

- Rnd 2 Ch 2, turn your work and going in the opposite direction, work 1 hdc in each st around, end slip st to top of first ch-2.

- Rnd 3 Ch 2, turn your work and going in the opposite direction (the same direction as in rnd 1), work 1 hdc in each st around, end slip st to top of first ch-2.

- Rnds 4 - 9 Rep rnds 2 - 3, remembering to turn and work each rnd in the opposite direction of the previous rnd. Piece should be approx 4"/10cm from beginning, slightly stretched.
Change to size K/6.5mm hook. Cont to turn work at beginning of each rnd.

- Next rnd Ch 3, work 1 dc in between first 2 hdc, then work 1 dc in between each hdc around; end slip st to top of first ch-3.

- Work 8 more rnds in dc, working in between sts of previous row.
Try on skirt at this point and note fit. It should measure approx 8"/20.5cm from beginning and fit along hip to top of fullest point of hip. If you want the fullness to begin a little higher on your hip line, rip back a rnd or two.

- Change to size L/8mm hook.

- Next rnd Ch 3 and working dc in between sts of previous rnd, [work 5 dc, then work 2 dc in between next 2 dc] 15 (15, 16, 17, 18) times, work 1 (4, 4, 4, 4) dc, 2 dc between last 2 sts; end slip to top of first ch-3 = 107 (112, 119, 126, 133) sts.

- Next 2 rnds Work in dc as for last rnd and increase sts on each rnd by working 2 dc in between the 2 increase dc of previous rnd and working 6 dc between increases on next round and 7 dc between increases on following round = 137 (144, 153, 162, 171) sts.

- Next 9 rnds Do not work increases any more. Work evenly around in dc, remembering to turn your work at beginning of each rnd.

Let the skirt hang out for a day or so and/or wash/dry the skirt. Try on skirt and decide on final skirt length. You want to end approx 2"/5cm before your final desired length. Rip back or work 1 or 2 more rnds as necessary.

FINAL 3 RNDS

• Change to size M/9mm hook.

• Next rnd Ch 2, work 1 hdc in between each st around, end slip st to top of first ch-2.

• Next rnd Ch 4, work 1 treble in between each st around, end slip st to top of first ch-4.

• Change to size K/6.5mm hook.

• Final rnd Ch 2, work 2 hdc between each st around, end slip st to top of first ch-2.

• Cut yarn and fasten off.

• Weave in ends. Sew first row closed at beginning of skirt.

MAKE DRAWSTRING

• With size K/6.5mm hook, chain a length that will fit comfortably around your waist with enough extra to tie into a small bow. Try on and make length longer or shorter as necessary. Turn and work 1 slip st in each chain to the end.

• Cut yarn and fasten off.

• Weave in ends. Weave drawstring through top of skirt and adjust to fit.

USING ELASTIC

Cut a length of 1"/2.5cm elastic in appropriate color to fit evenly around your waist, with approximately 1"/2.5cm extra at each end. Bear in mind that it must stretch to fit around your hips as you step into the skirt or around your shoulders and bust if you intend to pull the skirt over your head. Overlap the ends together and sew securely.
Pin the elastic evenly to skirt. Using herringbone stitch, sew elastic into position.

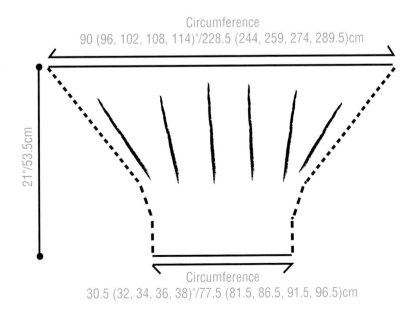

Circumference
90 (96, 102, 108, 114)"/228.5 (244, 259, 274, 289.5)cm

21"/53.5cm

Circumference
30.5 (32, 34, 36, 38)"/77.5 (81.5, 86.5, 91.5, 96.5)cm

SHRUGS

You'll never shrug off the practical beauty of these three designs! Crocheted of warm, soft yarn, they're just too magical to ignore. And even though they're "one size to fit most," I'm including instructions to give you a little more ease or to take up a little slack. Shrugs are just so nice to have around—your shoulders!

GEODE

■■□□ **EASY +**

TO FIT SIZES

• One size to fit most as written. Adjustments for back and sleeve cuff-to-sleeve cuff length are included in pattern.

FINISHED MEASUREMENTS

• Measured flat, approx 14"/35.5cm wide and 45"/114.5cm long (including border).

MATERIALS

Berroco® Geode®
(each ball approx 1.75oz/50g, 50% wool, 50% acrylic, 103yds/94m)
• 7 balls in #3644 Rainbow Agate
(1 or 2 balls more if you make the piece larger)
• Size K/6.5mm crochet hook.

GAUGE

• 16 sts and 8 rows to 4"/10cm in double crochet using size K/6.5mm hook.

NOTE

• Shrug is worked in one piece from one sleeve edge to the other.

"Nobody can be exactly like me.
Even I have trouble doing it!"
—Tallulah Bankhead

SHRUG
FIRST (LOWER) PART OF SHRUG

• With size K/6.5mm hook, ch 32.

• Row 1 Work 1 dc in 4th ch from hook, *ch 1, skip 1 dc, work 1 dc in next ch; repeat from* across = 14 ch-1 spaces. Turn.

• Row 2 Ch 3, *work 1 dc in ch-1 sp, ch 1; repeat from* across, end 1 dc in between final two sts of previous row. Turn.

• Repeat row 2 until piece measures 44"/112cm from beginning. If you want the piece longer than this (from cuff to cuff), work more rows until piece is 1"/2.5cm shorter than your desired length.

SECOND (UPPER) PART OF SHRUG

• Row 1 Working along one long edge of first part, ch 2, work 1 hdc around stem of first dc, *ch 1, work 1 hdc around stem of next dc; repeat from* across, end 1 hdc around stem of final dc. Before turning the work, mark this side of shrug as the right side of the garment. Turn.

• Row 2 Ch 2, *work 1 hdc in ch-1 sp, ch 1; repeat from* across, end 1 hdc in between final 2 sts of previous row. Turn.

• Repeat row 2 until second part measures approx 6.5"/16.5cm from beginning, or approx 13"/33cm wide.

• If you want the second part (bodice) to be wider, work more rows in this section until desired width.

• Cut yarn and fasten off.

FINISHING

• Folding piece in half, sew or crochet approx 10"/25.5cm on either side for sleeve seams.

• Try on to check fit. If you prefer a tighter fit around bodice, sew a little more at each sleeve seam. If you need more room, let each sleeve seam out a bit.

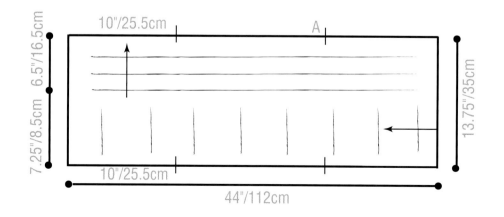

"Fashion fades, only style remains the same."
—Coco Chanel

COLLAR

- With right side of garment facing you, join yarn to corner sp of second part of shrug (point A on schematic).

- Row 1 Ch 4 (counts as 1 dc and ch 1), 1 dc in next ch-1 sp, *ch 1, 1 dc in next ch-1 sp; repeat from* across to final ch-1 sp just before sleeve seam. Turn.

- Row 2 Ch 4, skip first ch-1 sp, *dc in next ch-1 sp, ch 1; repeat from* across, end dc in final ch-1 space. Turn.

- Repeat row 2 until collar measures approx 6.5"/16.5cm from beginning (a total of about 13 rows).

- Cut yarn and fasten off.

RUFFLE AROUND COLLAR EDGE

- With the right side of garment facing you and working around stem of hdc and in ch-1 sps, join yarn to first sp at bottom corner of collar and ch 8, sc in same first sp, *ch 8, sc in next sp, ch 8, sc in same space; repeat from* around collar.

- Cut yarn and fasten off.

LOWER BODICE AND SLEEVE BORDERS

- Row 1 With the right side of garment facing you, join yarn to lower edge of bodice, ch 2 and work 1 row sc evenly across. Do not turn.

- Row 2 Ch 2, work 1 row reverse single crochet.

- Cut yarn and fasten off.

- In same way, repeat rows 1-2 around each sleeve edge, joining to first stitch with slip stitch at the end of each rnd.

- Weave in ends.

IVY LEAGUE

◀️■☐☐ **EASY**

TO FIT SIZES

• One size to fit most as written. Adjustments for back and sleeve cuff-to-sleeve cuff length are included in pattern.

FINISHED MEASUREMENTS

• Measured flat, approx 20"/51cm wide and 68"/172.5cm long.

MATERIALS

Red Heart® Collage™

(each skein approx 3.5oz/100g, 100% acrylic, 218yds/200m)
• 4 skeins in #2407 Ice Storm
• One each sizes J/6mm and K/6.5mm crochet hooks.

GAUGE

• 16 sts and 6 rows to 4"/10cm in pattern using size K/6.5mm crochet hook.

NOTES

• This shrug is worked as a large rectangle which is folded in half and the side edges are sewn to form sleeves.
• The yarn stripes in tones of grey. No attempt was made to match stripes from one ball to another. We used one ball, then moved to the 2nd and so on.

SHRUG
FIRST STRIPE

With size K/6.5mm hook, ch 67. (To add or subtract width, add or subtract in increments of 4. For example, ch 59 or 63 or 71 or 75. Each 4-st increment will equal 1"/2.5cm.)

• Foundation row Work (2 dc, ch 1, 1 dc) in 4th ch from hook, *skip 3 ch, work (3 dc, ch 1, 1 dc) in next ch; repeat from* across to last 3 ch, end skip 2 ch, 1 dc in last ch. Before turning the work, mark this side of shrug as the right side of the garment. Turn.

• Row 1 Ch 3, work (2 dc, ch 1, 1 dc) in first ch-1 sp, *work (3 dc, ch 1, 1 dc) in each ch-1 sp across, end 1 dc in top of first st of preceding row. Turn.

• Repeat row 1 a total of 8 times more. Including foundation row, 10 rows in pattern have been worked. Piece is approx 7"/18cm from beginning, slightly stretched.

SECOND STRIPE

• Row 1 *Ch 5, sc in between the first 2 motifs of previous row (the 3dc-ch1-1dc motifs; you can see this clearly on the photo); repeat from* across, end ch 5, sc in top of first st of previous row. Turn.

• Rows 2 - 5 Ch 5, sc in first ch-5 space, then work ch 5, sc in each ch-5 space across. Turn.
The 5 rows measure approx 3"/7.5cm, measured flat.

THIRD STRIPE

• Row 1 Ch 3, in first ch-5 sp work (2 dc, ch 1, 1 dc), *work (3 dc, ch 1, 1 dc) in each ch-5 sp across, end 1 dc in top of first st of preceding row. Turn.

• Rows 2 - 10 Rep row 1 of first stripe.

FOURTH STRIPE

• Repeat 5 rows of second stripe.

FIFTH STRIPE

• Drape a tape measure around your neck and let it hang along your shoulders and arms down to your wrists. This will give you your approximate 'wingspan' measurement. Compare this to the length of your rectangle (68"/172.5cm). If you want a shorter wingspan, work fewer rows in this (middle) section. For example, working 3 rows less would equal a 2"/5cm shorter piece. Our model has very long arms and liked the length of this shrug. You can also fold the sleeve edges back to form cuffs and tack in position.

• Repeat row 1 of third stripe. Continue as for first stripe until you've worked approximately 28"/71cm in pattern. Our sample has 40 rows. (Work more or less rows as desired.)

SIXTH AND EIGHTH STRIPE

• Work 5 rows of second stripe.

SEVENTH AND NINTH STRIPE

• Work 10 rows of third stripe.

• Cut yarn and fasten off.

FINISHING

• Wash piece and lay flat to dry.

• Mark the center 22"/56cm on each long edge for bodice opening. Using schematic as guide, fold piece in half widthwise and sew points A-B to B-A on each side for sleeve seams.

BORDER

• Rnd 1 With right side of garment facing and size J/6mm hook, join yarn to corner of one sleeve seam, ch 3 and work in dc evenly around, end slip st to top of first ch-3 to join.

• Try piece on to see if you need to decrease some stitches on next round to tighten border.

• Rnd 2 Ch 2, work 1 hdc in each dc around, decreasing evenly if necessary for proper fit.

• Rnd 3 Ch 2, work around in reverse single crochet.

• Cut yarn and fasten off.

• Weave in ends.

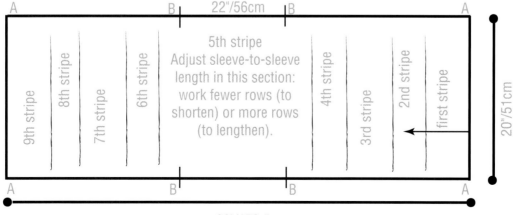

HEX ON

■■■□ INTERMEDIATE

TO FIT SIZES

• One size to fit up to 46"/117cm bust (measured above bustline, at underarm).

• Center back length approx 13"/33cm.

MATERIALS

Noro Taiyo

(each ball approx 3.5oz/100g, 40% cotton, 30% silk, 15% wool, 15% nylon, 218yds/200m)

• 3 balls in #4 Yellows, Rusts, Pinks

• Size K/6.5mm crochet hook.

• Optional: two $1^3/_8$"/34mm buttons (buttons shown in sample are from designer's personal collection).

GAUGE

• 11 sts to 4"/10cm and 6 rows to 3.5"/9cm in double crochet using size K/6.5mm crochet hook.

• Each hexagon is approx 7"/18cm wide.

NOTES

• Shrug is worked in hexagons that are sewn together.

• To adjust for larger size, read through the paragraph just before finishing instructions on page 67.

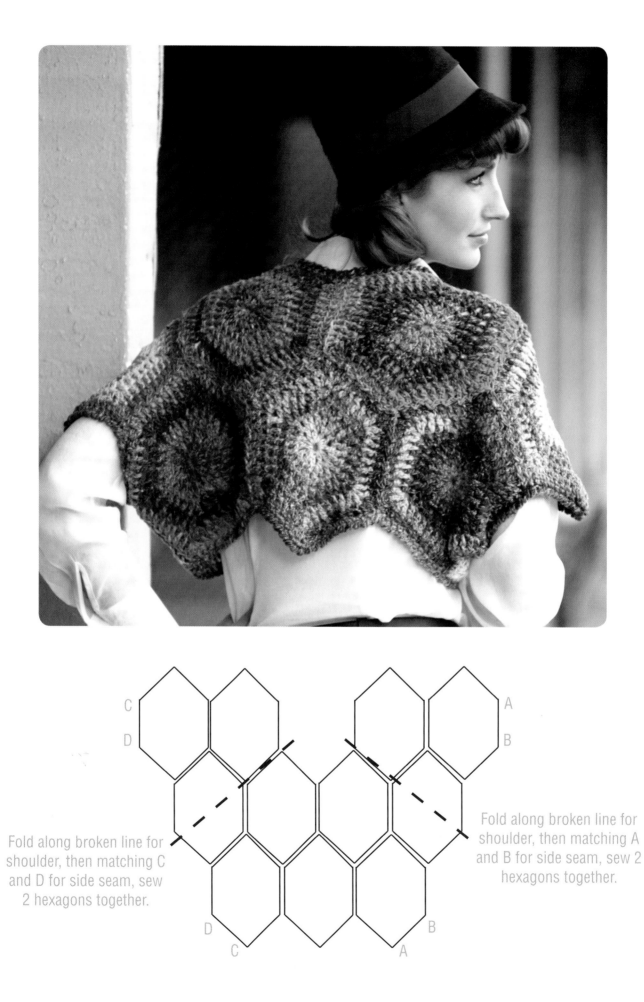

Fold along broken line for shoulder, then matching C and D for side seam, sew 2 hexagons together.

Fold along broken line for shoulder, then matching A and B for side seam, sew 2 hexagons together.

SHRUG
HEXAGON (MAKE 11)

- With size K/6.5mm hook, ch 4, then join with slip st to form a ring.

- Rnd 1 Ch 3, work 11 dc in ring, end slip st to top of first ch-3 to join. Do not turn at end of this or any following rnd. Mark this side of hexagon as the right side.

- Rnd 2 Ch 3 (counts as 1 dc), [work 2 dc in between 2 sts of previous rnd] 11 times, end 1 dc in between final 2 sts, slip st to top of first ch-3 to join = 24 dc.

- Rnd 3 Ch 3, working in between each dc of previous rnd, *work 3 dc, then work (1 dc, ch 1, 1 dc) in between next 2 sts for corner sp; repeat from* 5 times, end last repeat 1 dc in final sp, ch 1, slip st to top of first ch-3 = 6 corner sps.

- Rnd 4 Ch 3, working in between each dc of previous rnd, *work 4 dc, then work (1 dc, ch 1, 1 dc) in ch-1 corner sp; repeat from* around, end 1 dc in final corner sp, ch 1, slip st to top of first ch-3.

- Rnd 5 Ch 3, work 1 dc in same corner, working in between each dc of previous rnd, *work 5 dc, then work (2 dc, ch 1, 2 dc) in corner ch-1 sp; repeat from* around, end 2 dc in final corner sp, ch 1, slip st to top of first ch-3.

- Rnd 6 Ch 3, work 1 dc in same corner, working in between each dc of previous rnd, *work 8 dc, then work (2 dc, ch 1, 2 dc) in corner ch-1 sp; repeat from* around, end 2 dc in final corner sp, ch 1, slip st to top of first ch-3.

- Cut yarn and fasten off.

- Using schematic as guide and contrasting yarn (for ease in ripping), baste hexagons together, including side seams. Try on and decide on fit. Add 1 or 2 rows of dc along the side seams (2 marked A-B and 2 marked C-D). For an overall larger size, add a 7th rnd of sc or dc to each hexagon, then follow finishing instructions below.

FINISHING

- Block hexagons lightly or handwash, then lay flat to dry.

- Using schematic as guide, sew hexagons together.

FINAL BORDER
(To tighten fit along lower edge, decrease as necessary OR use smaller hook.)

- With right side of garment facing, join yarn and work 1 rnd in sc, then 1 rnd in reverse sc evenly around neckline, lower and front edges and each armhole.

- Cut yarn and fasten off.

- Weave in ends.

- Optional: Work 2 buttonloops in sc evenly spaced on right front, each approx 1"/2.5cm long. Sew buttons on left front.

VESTS

Whether playing it close or letting it flow, a vest always takes your mode of dress to the next level. Here are four ways to put color and texture where you want it. You're about to see vests as you've never seen them before, and I hope you love all four styles as much as I do!

WILD FLOWERS

■■□□ EASY +

TO FIT SIZES
- X-Small, Small, Medium, Large, X-Large
- Shown in size X-Small.

FINISHED MEASUREMENTS
(Both bust and length are given with piece measured flat. Note that there is at least 6-8"/15-20.5cm worth of ease in bust size when worn.)
- Bust 32 (34, 35.5, 37, 38)"/81.5 (86.5, 90, 94, 96.5)cm
- Length (measured flat)
  18 (19, 20, 22.5, 22.5)"/45.5 (48.5, 51, 57, 57)cm

MATERIALS
Tahki Cotton Classic

(each skein approx 1.75oz/50g, 100% mercerized cotton, 108yds/100m)
- Main Color: 6 (6, 7, 7, 8) skeins in #3002 Black

Tahki Pansy

(each ball approx .8oz/25g, 100% nylon, 163yds/150m)
- Main Color: 4 (4, 5, 5, 5) balls in #008 Black/Red/Fuchsia/Blue
- Size K/6.5mm and size I/5.5mm crochet hooks.

GAUGE
- 9 sts and 7 rows to 4"/10cm in double crochet (worked in between stitches) using size K/6.5mm crochet hook and 1 strand of each yarn held together.

NOTES

• Vest is worked in one piece from lower edge to top of neckline. It is meant to be worn open.

• Body of vest is worked with 1 strand of each yarn held together. Trim is worked with 1 strand of solid color only.

• After first row, work double crochet stitches in between stitches of previous row.

VEST

• With size K/6.5mm hook and 1 strand of each yarn held together, ch 74 (78, 81, 85, 88).

• Row 1 Work 1 dc in 4th chain from hook, then in each chain across = 72 (76, 79, 82, 85) dc.

• Rows 2 - 10 (11, 11, 12, 12) Ch 3 (counts as 1 dc), turn and work 1 dc in between each st across. Including your first ch 3, you will have the same number of dc in each row.

Piece measures approx 5.75 (6.25, 6.25, 7, 7)"/14.5 (16, 16, 18, 18)cm from beginning, slightly stretched.

Lengthen piece at this point by working a few more rows until desired length to underarm.

• Divide for armhole: Next row Ch 3 (counts as first st), turn and work 19 (20, 21, 22, 23) more stitches. Cut yarn and fasten off. These 20 (21, 22, 23, 24) sts will form the right front.

• Join yarn in between next 2 sts, ch 3 (counts as first st) and work 31 (33, 34, 35, 36) more sts. This is the back of vest. Before turning the work, mark this side of vest as the right side of the garment.

• Turn work and continue pattern for 15 (15, 17, 17, 17) rows more.

• Cut yarn and fasten off.

LEFT FRONT

• With right side of the garment facing you, join yarn to left side of back in between next 2 sts (point A on schematic), ch 3 and continue double crochet pattern across = 20 (21, 22, 23, 24) sts.

• Work 15 (15, 17, 17, 17) rows more.

• Cut yarn and fasten off.

RIGHT FRONT

• With wrong side of garment facing you, join yarn in between first 2 sts of right front (point B on schematic). Ch 3 and continue pattern for 15 (15, 17, 17, 17) rows more.

• Cut yarn and fasten off.

• Right front, back and left front each have a total of 16 (16, 18, 18, 18) rows from beginning of armhole.

• Tack top of front and back armholes together (at points C on schematic) and try on to make sure armholes are deep enough. If necessary, work a few more rows to each front and back to lengthen armhole.

JOIN 2 FRONTS AND BACK

• Next (joining) row (RS) With the right side of garment facing you, begin at right front edge (point D on schematic), join yarn to top of first st, ch 3 and continue in pattern across.

• Work 5 (7, 7, 9, 9) rows more.

• Cut yarn and fasten off.

FINISHING

• Block piece lightly OR hand wash piece and dry flat. Weave in ends.

• With size I/5.5 hook, right side of garment facing and 1 strand of solid color, join yarn to upper right corner (point E on schematic), ch 2 and work 1 sc in each st across. Do not turn work. Ch 2 and work 1 row reverse single crochet evenly across.

• Cut yarn and fasten off.

• In same way, work trim along lower edge of piece and around each armhole. Try on and fold front edges back to form V-shaped lapels. Tack into position as desired.

Notice that the armhole opens up quite a bit even though it's just a slit within the rectangle.

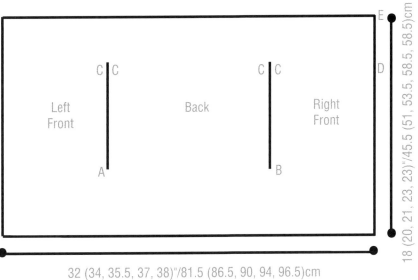

Left Front   Back   Right Front

18 (20, 21, 23, 23)"/45.5 (51, 53.5, 58.5, 58.5)cm

32 (34, 35.5, 37, 38)"/81.5 (86.5, 90, 94, 96.5)cm

DARK ANGEL

◖◼◻◻ **EASY +**

TO FIT SIZES

• One size to fit most with sizing adjustments made for shoulder width and armhole depth.

FINISHED MEASUREMENTS

• Measured flat, approx 29"/73.5cm along shorter edge and 51"/129.5cm along longer edge.

MATERIALS

Caron® Simply Soft® Tweed

(each skein approx 3oz/85g, 96% acrylic, 4% rayon, 150yds/137m)
• 9 skeins in #0010 Black
• 1 skein in #0007 Autumn Red
• One each size H/5mm and I/5.5mm crochet hooks.

GAUGE

• 13 sts and 8 rows to 4"/10cm in double crochet using size H/5mm crochet hook.

Another very easy, rectangular shape.

Approached from different angles,

its asymmetric swirls skim the body beautifully.

NOTES

- Vest is worked as a traditional granny square, begun in the center (C on schematic) and worked in rounds of double crochet.
- Front panels are then crocheted back and forth in rows at each side of the square to form a rectangle.

VEST

- With size H/5mm hook and Black, ch 5, then join with slip st to form a ring.

- Rnd 1 Ch 3, work 2 dc in ring, *ch 2, work 3 dc in ring; repeat from* twice more, ch 2, slip st to top of first ch-3.

- Rnd 2 Ch 3, work 1 dc in same ch-2 sp, *work 1 dc in each of next 3 dc, work (2 dc-ch 2-2 dc) in ch-2 sp; repeat from* around, end by working 2 dc in final ch-2 sp, ch 2, slip st to top of first ch-3.

- Rnd 3 Ch 3, work 1 dc in same ch-2 sp, *work 1 dc in each dc to next ch-2 sp, work (2 dc-ch 2-2 dc) in ch-2 sp; repeat from* around, end by working 2 dc in final ch-2 sp, ch 2, slip st to top of first ch-3.

- Repeat rnd 3 as follows:

  - For very narrow shoulders, work until piece is approx 13"/33cm across top of piece, or approx 13 rnds total from the beginning.

  - For average shoulders, work until piece is approx 14-15"/35.5-38cm across top of piece, or approx 14 to 15 rnds total from the beginning.

  - For wide shoulders, work until piece is approx 16"/40.5cm across top of piece, or approx 16 rnds total from the beginning.

- Hold the piece up to your shoulder line to determine correct width for your body type. Work fewer or more rounds as necessary, ending at a corner.

- Beginning on the 5th st, mark:
  30 sts (narrow armhole)
  32 sts (average armhole)
  34 sts (deeper armhole) along 2 opposite sides of piece (points A and B on schematic).

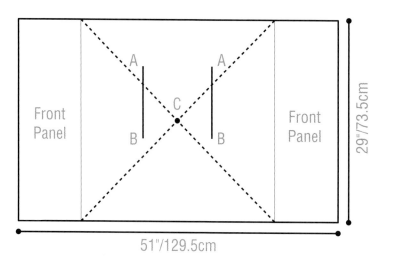

SHAPE ARMHOLE

- Next rnd Ch 3, work 1 dc in same ch-2 sp, work 1 dc in each st to marked st, then ch 30 or 32 or 34 (depending on your markers), skip the next 30 or 32 or 34 marked sts and continue pattern around to opposite marked sts, then ch 30 or 32 or 34 and skip the marked sts, then continue around in pattern.

- On the following rnd, work 1 dc in each of the 30 or 32 or 34 ch of previous rnd.

- Continue in pattern until the piece has a total of 29 rnds from the beginning, or piece measures approx 29"/73.5cm along one side (measuring piece flat).

- Cut yarn and fasten off.

- Try piece on at this point. The armholes are closer to the top, or collar edge. Use photo as guide and fold collar edge as desired. You will be adding approx 11"/28cm more fabric to each side of both fronts.

FRONT PANELS

- With right side of garment facing you, join yarn to one corner ch-2 sp, ch 3 and work 1 dc in each st across, ending 1 dc in ch-2 sp. Turn work.

- Ch 3 at beginning of each row and work evenly in rows of dc for approx 11"/28cm or about 22 rows total.

- Cut yarn and fasten off.

- Try on as you go along and work more or less rows as desired for a personal fit.

- In same way, work panel on opposite side to match first panel.

FINISHING

- Work borders with right side of garment facing you and size I/5.5mm hook. Cut yarn and fasten off after each rnd is complete.

- Rnd 1 Join Black to any corner, *ch 3, skip 1 dc, sc in next dc; rep from* around piece, end slip st to first st of first ch-3 to join.

- Rnd 2 Join Red to any ch-3 sp, *ch 3, remove hook from st (leaving it open), then insert hook from front to back through next ch-3 sp and into open st, pull it through the sp, then repeat from* around, end slip st to first ch-3 to join.

- Rnd 3 Join Black to any ch-3 sp and repeat from* of rnd 2.

- In same way, work rnds 1 and 2 around each armhole, using Red for rnd 1 and Black for rnd 2.

- Weave in ends.

MINI ME

◖■☐▢ **EASY**

TO FIT SIZES

- X-Small, Small, Medium, Large, X-Large
- Shown in size X-Small.

FINISHED MEASUREMENTS

- Bust 34.5 (37.5, 40.5, 42.5, 45)"/ 87.5 (95.5, 103, 108, 114.5)cm
- Length (measured when worn)
  13 (13, 13.5, 13.5, 13.5)"/ 33 (33, 34.5, 34.5, 34.5)cm

MATERIALS

Muench Yarns Oceana

(each ball approx 1.75oz/50g, 55% viscose, 30% nylon, 15% cotton, 77yds/70m)

- 3 (3, 3, 4, 4) balls in #4802 Queen Green
- Size K/6.5mm crochet hook.
- Optional: two ¾"/19mm buttons.
- Optional: Dritz® Fray Check™.

GAUGE

- 11 sts and 5 rows to 4"/10cm in double crochet using size K/6.5mm crochet hook.

NOTES

- Vest is worked in one piece to underarm, then divided for fronts and back.
- Gauge is given in double crochet as it is easier to measure than chain net stitch.
- The fabric is very stretchy. The armholes will open up easily and stretch to fit.

VEST

- Ch 97 (105, 113, 119, 125).

- Work 1 dc in 4th ch from hook and in each ch across = 95 (103, 111, 117, 123) dc.

For sizes Medium, Large and X-Large only:
- Turn, ch 3 and work 1 dc in each st across.

For all sizes:
- Row 1 *Ch 3, skip 1 dc, sc in next dc; repeat from* across = 47 (51, 55, 58, 61) ch-3 sps. Turn.

- Rows 2-5 Ch 3, sc in first ch-3 sp, *ch 3, sc in next ch-3 sp; repeat from* across. Turn.

DIVIDE FOR UNDERARM

- Turn after row 5 and mark the side that's facing you as the right side of the garment. From here until the finish, all even rows are the right side of garment rows.

- Count 11 (12, 13, 14, 15) ch-3 sps, mark the next ch-3 sp, count 23 (25, 27, 28, 29) ch-3 sps and mark the next ch-3 sp.

  - First 11 (12, 13, 14, 15) ch-3 sps are the right front

  - 1 marked sp is the underarm

  - The center 23 (25, 27, 28, 29) sps are the back

  - 1 marked sp is the underarm

  - Final 11 (12, 13, 14, 15) ch-3 sps are the left front.

- Row 6 Ch 3, sc in first ch-3 sp, *ch 3, sc in next ch-3 sp; repeat from* until the first marked ch-3 sp; leaving marked sp open. Turn.

FINISH THE RIGHT FRONT AS FOLLOWS:

- Row 7 Ch 3, sc in first ch-3 sp, *ch 3, sc in next ch-3 sp; repeat from* across. Turn.

Because the pattern stitch is very malleable, when worn, it looks as though there's neck shaping. As you can see from the schematic, the only shaping is done at each underarm.

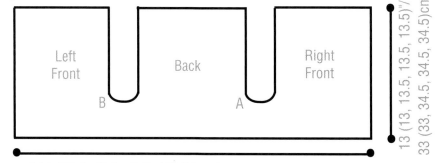

34.5 (37.5, 40.5, 42.5, 45)"/87.5 (95.5, 103, 108, 114.5)cm

- **Row 8** Ch 3, sc in first ch-3 sp, *ch 3, sc in next ch-3 sp; repeat from* across to last 2 ch-3 sps and do not work into them. Turn.

- **Row 9** Ch 3, sc in first ch-3 sp, *ch 3, sc in next ch-3 sp; repeat from* across. Turn.

- **Rows 10 - 22** Rep row 2.

- Cut yarn and fasten off.

BACK

- With right side of garment facing you, join yarn to ch-3 sp immediately after first marked ch-3 sp (point A on schematic). Ch 3, and work row 2 across to next marked ch-3 sp; leaving marked sp open. Turn.

- **Next 2 rows** Ch 3, skip first ch-3 sp and sc in next ch-3 sp, *ch 3, sc in next ch-3 sp; repeat from* across to last ch-3 sp and leaving last sp open. Turn.

- **Rows 9 - 22** Repeat row 2.

- Cut yarn and fasten off.

LEFT FRONT

- With right side of garment facing you, join yarn to ch-3 sp immediately after 2nd marked ch-3 sp (point B on schematic). Ch 3, and work in pattern across. Turn.

- **Next row** Ch 3, sc in first ch-3 sp, *ch 3, sc in next ch-3 sp; repeat from* across, leaving last sp open. Turn.

- **Next row** Ch 3, sc in first ch-3 sp, *ch 3, sc in next ch-3 sp; repeat from* across. Turn.

- **Rows 9 - 22** Complete as for left front by repeating row 2.

- Cut yarn and fasten off.

FINISHING

- Working from armhole edge in towards neckline, sew or crochet shoulders together, approx 3.5"/9cm along shoulder line. Before cutting yarn, try on and make any necessary adjustments.

NECK RUFFLE

- With right side of garment facing you, join yarn to first ch-3 sp at right front neck edge, ch 5, sc in same sp, ch 5, sc in same sp again, *ch 5, sc in next sp, ch 5, sc in same sp; repeat from* across.

- Cut yarn and fasten off.

LOWER EDGE

- With right side of garment facing you, join yarn to lower edge of right front, ch 2 and working in between each dc, work 1 row reverse single crochet evenly along lower edge.

- Use a liquid seam sealant on ends if desired. Weave in ends.

Optional: Sew 2 buttons at top of left front as desired. Use open ch-3 sps on opposite side as buttonholes.

SWEET BASIL

 ◼◼◻◻ **EASY +**

TO FIT SIZES
- X-Small, Small, Medium, Large, X-Large
- Shown in size Small.

FINISHED MEASUREMENTS
- Bust 32 (36, 40, 44, 48)"/ 81.5 (91.5, 101.5, 112, 122)cm
- Length (measured flat)
      21 (22, 22, 23, 23)"/ 53.5 (56, 56, 58.5, 58.5)cm

MATERIALS

Berroco® Trilogy™
(each skein approx 1.75oz/50g, 32% wool, 28% cotton, 40% nylon, 80yds/74m)
- 8 (8, 9, 9, 10) skeins in #7634 Aberdeen

Berroco® Pure® Merino DK
(each ball approx 1.75oz/50g, 100% extra fine merino, 126yds/115m)
- 1 skein in #4542 Kale
- One each sizes H/5mm and K/6.5mm crochet hooks.
- Optional: Dritz® Fray Check™.

GAUGE
- 11 sts and 7 rows to 4"/10cm in double crochet using Trilogy and size K/6.5mm crochet hook.

The deep armhole makes for easy layering. Here, the vest was layered over the suede shirt instead of under it— for some bragging rights!

NOTES

• Vest is worked from side to side in one piece.
• The initial foundation chain will determine the length of the piece.
• The piece will be approx 1"/2.5cm longer when worn.

VEST

• With size K/6.5mm hook, ch 57 (61, 61, 65, 65).

• Row 1 Work 1 dc in 3rd ch from hook, *ch 1, skip 1 ch, 1 dc in next ch; repeat from* across = 27 (29, 29, 31, 31) ch-1 sps. The ch 2 (before the first dc at the beginning of the row) is a turning ch and is not part of any stitch count, before turning the work, mark this side of the vest as the right side of the garment. Turn at end of this and every row.

• Row 2 Ch 2 (this is a turning ch, work this at the beginning of all following rows), work 1 dc in each dc and ch-1 sp across = 55 (59, 59, 63, 63) dc.

• Row 3 Work 1 dc in each dc across.

• Row 4 (eyelet row) Work 1 dc in first dc, *ch 1, skip 1 dc, work 1 dc in next dc; repeat from* across.

• Rows 5 - 7 Work 3 rows in dc.

• Row 8 Repeat row 4 (eyelet row).

• Work 4 (6, 8, 6, 6) rows more in dc. Piece measures approx 6.5 (8, 9, 8, 8)"/16.5 (20.5, 23, 20.5, 20.5)cm from beginning.

SHAPE ARMHOLE

• Next row Work 25 (29, 29, 33, 33) dc. Turn.

• Work 3 (3, 5, 7, 11) rows more in dc on these sts only, ending at point A on schematic. Turn.

• Next row Work 25 (29, 29, 33, 33) dc, then ch 32 (30 plus 2 sts for the turning ch). Turn.

• Next row Work 1 dc in 3rd ch from hook, then in each ch across, then in each dc across = 55 (59, 59, 63, 63) dc.

• Work 4 (6, 6, 8, 8) rows more in dc, end at point B on schematic.

• Work 12-row eyelet panel as follows:
    repeat row 4 (eyelet row),
    work 2 rows in dc
    repeat row 4 (eyelet row)
    work 4 rows in dc
    repeat row 4 (eyelet row)
    work 2 rows in dc
    repeat row 4 (eyelet row), ending at
        point C on schematic.

• Work 5 (7, 7, 9, 9) rows more in dc, ending at point D on schematic.

• Cut yarn and fasten off.

SHAPE 2ND ARMHOLE

• With wrong side facing, skip first 30 sts and join yarn to next st, ch 2, work 1 dc in same st and in each dc across.

• Work 3 (3, 5, 7, 11) rows more in dc on these sts only.

• Cut yarn and fasten off.

- Next row Ch 30, with wrong side facing, work 1 dc in each dc across, ending at point E on schematic.

- Next row Work 1 dc in each dc, then in each ch across = 55 (59, 59, 63, 63) dc.

- Work 3 (5, 7, 5, 5) rows more in dc, end at point F on schematic.

- Work final 8 rows as follows:
  - repeat row 4 (eyelet row)
  - work 3 rows in dc
  - repeat row 4 (eyelet row)
  - work 2 rows in dc
  - repeat row 4 (eyelet row), ending at point G on schematic.

- Cut yarn and fasten off.

FINISHING

- Block piece lightly.

- Use a liquid seam sealer on yarn ends if desired. Weave in ends.

- Working from armhole edge towards neck, sew or crochet 4 (4.5, 5, 5, 5)"/10 (11.5, 12.5, 12.5, 12.5)cm along each shoulder seam.

TRIM

- Work all trim with size H/5 crochet hook, solid colored yarn and the right side of the garment facing you.

- Around each armhole: Join yarn to middle of underarm, ch 2 and work 1 rnd of sc evenly around armhole, ending slip st to top of first ch-2 to join.

- At front edges: Join yarn to lower right front (or upper left front), ch 2 and work 1 sc in each dc, 2 sc in each ch-1 space.

- At neck edge, join yarn to right front neck edge, ch 2 and work evenly in sc around to left front neck edge.

- At lower edge, join yarn, ch 2 and work 1 row sc evenly across lower edge. Do not turn. Ch 2 and work 1 row reverse single crochet.

- Cut yarn and fasten off.

Feel free to play with the eyelets.
Add buttons and use them as buttonholes.
Stab a shawl pin or decorative hairpin or even a crochet hook through the eyelets to close the vest.
Thread ribbon or suede or leather strips through front and back eyelets for more contrasting textures.

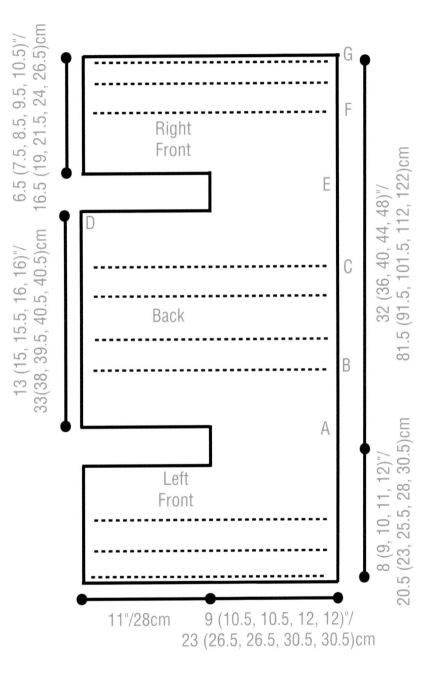

Right
Front

Back

Left
Front

G

F

E

D

C

B

A

6.5 (7.5, 8.5, 9.5, 10.5)"/
16.5 (19, 21.5, 24, 26.5)cm

13 (15, 15.5, 16, 16)"/
33(38, 39.5, 40.5, 40.5)cm

32 (36, 40, 44, 48)"/
81.5 (91.5, 101.5, 112, 122)cm

8 (9, 10, 11, 12)"/
20.5 (23, 25.5, 28, 30.5)cm

11"/28cm

9 (10.5, 10.5, 12, 12)"/
23 (26.5, 26.5, 30.5, 30.5)cm

HATS

Hat people, rejoice! These five hats (one with a variation for really plush yarn—so make that six!) are super easy to crochet. From an artistically draped beret to a quick helmet with matching neckband and wristlets, you'll find your favorite cold-weather accessories here. Wear them with unexpected outfits or use them to add color and confidence to your conventional outerwear. If you think you're not a hat person, then you must make one of these beauties! Your true personality is just waiting for the moment you try it on!

THE BLUES

 EASY

FINISHED SIZE

• Headband circumference approx 17"/43cm.

MATERIALS

Araucania Nature Wool Chunky Multi 🧶 **BULKY 5**

(each approx 3.5oz/100g, 100% wool, 132yds/120m)

• 1 skein in color #207 Blues

• One each sizes J/6mm and K/6.5mm crochet hooks.

GAUGE

• 10 sts to 4"/10cm and 4 rows to 3"/7.5cm in double crochet using size K/6.5mm hook.

No tears here — so easy to make, so easy to wear.

BERET

- With size K/6.5mm hook, ch 4. Join with slip st to form ring.

- Rnd 1 Ch 3 (this counts as 1 dc in this and every round), then work 11 dc in ring = 12 dc. Slip st to top of first ch-3 to join; do this at end of each round. Do not turn your work. Continue to work around with the same side always facing you.

- Rnd 2 Ch 3, work 1 dc in same st, then work 2 dc in each dc around = 24 dc.

- Rnd 3 Ch 3, work 1 dc in same st, work 1 dc in next dc, *work 2 dc in next dc, work 1 dc in next dc; rep from* around = 36 dc.

- Rnd 4 Ch 3, work 1 dc in same st, work 1 dc in each of next 2 dc, *work 2 dc in next dc, work 1 dc in each of next 2 dc; rep from* around = 48 dc.

- Rnd 5 Ch 3, work 1 dc in same st, work 1 dc in each of next 3 dc, *work 2 dc in next dc, work 1 dc in each of next 3 dc; rep from* around = 60 dc.

- Rnd 6 Ch 3, work 1 dc in same st, work 1 dc in each of next 4 dc, *work 2 dc in next dc, work 1 dc in each of next 4 dc; rep from* around = 72 dc.

- Rnd 7 Ch 3, work 1 dc in same st, work 1 dc in each of next 5 dc, *work 2 dc in next dc, work 1 dc in each of next 5 dc; rep from* around = 84 dc.

Piece measures approx 11"/28cm across.

This is the widest point of hat. If you want it even wider, work another round or 2 of increases. If you want it narrower, work only through rnds 5 or 6.

- Rnd 8 Ch 3, then work 1 dc in each dc around.

- Change to size J/6mm hook.

- Rnds 9 - 13 Ch 3, then work 1 dc in each dc around.

- Rnd 14 Ch 3, *work 1 hdc over next 2 dc as foll: yo, go through st and draw up a loop, yo and through 2 loops (2 loops left on hook), yo again and go through next st and draw up a loop, yo and through all 4 loops on hook, work 1 hdc in next dc; rep from* around = 56 sts.

- Rnd 15 Ch 2, work 1 hdc in each hdc around.

- Rnds 16 - 19 Ch 2, then working in back loop only of each st, work 1 hdc in each hdc around.

- Rnd 20 Ch 2, work 1 rnd of reverse sc evenly around.

- Cut yarn and fasten off.

- Weave in yarn ends. Use yarn tail to close top of beret.

DOUBLE TAKE DOUBLE

(shown on page 94) **EASY**

FINISHED SIZE

- cap Approx 20"/51cm around and 7"/18cm deep.
- wristlets Approx 8"/20.5 around by 5"/12.5cm long.
- neckband Approx 3"/7.5cm wide by 19.5"/49.5cm long.

MATERIALS

SUPER BULKY 6

Classic Elite Aspen

(each approx 3.5oz/100g, 50% alpaca, 50% wool, 51yds/47m)

- 3 balls in color #1581 Tree Grove
- Size S/17mm crochet hook.
- 1.5"/38mm button.

GAUGE

- 4 sts and 2 rows to 3"/7.5cm in double crochet using size S/17mm hook.

Whichever way you choose to wear this helmet —
front to back or vice versa —
you'll catch second glances coming and going!

HELMET

- With size S/17mm hook, ch 5. Join with slip st to form ring.

- Rnd 1 Ch 3 (this counts as 1 dc in this and every round), then work 8 dc in ring = 9 dc. Slip st to top of first ch-3 to join; do this at end of each round. Do not turn. Continue to work around with the same side always facing you until end of row 5.

- Rnd 2 Ch 3, work 1 dc in same st, then work 2 dc in each dc around = 18 dc.

- Rnd 3 Ch 3, work 1 dc in same st, work 1 dc in each of next 2 dc, *work 2 dc in next dc, work 1 dc in each of next 2 dc; repeat from* around = 24 dc.

- Rnd 4 Ch 3, work 1 dc in each st around.

- Row 5 Ch 3, work 1 dc in each of next 17 dc. Turn.

- Row 6 Ch 3, work 1 dc in each st across. Turn.

- Row 7 Ch 1, then work slip st evenly across all sts.

- Cut yarn and fasten off.

- Weave in ends. Use yarn tail to close top of helmet.

THE EASIEST WRISTLETS

With size S/17mm hook, ch 12.

- Row 1 Work 1 dc in 4th ch from hook (the first 3 ch counts as 1 dc), then in each ch across = 10 dc. Slip st to top of first ch-3 to form a ring of dc, being careful not to twist ring.

- Rnds 1 - 2 Ch 3 (this counts as 1 dc), work 1 dc in each dc around. Slip st to top of first ch-3 to join. Do not turn. Continue to work around with same side facing you.

- Cut yarn and fasten off.

- Weave in ends. Use yarn tail to join lower edge together.

NECKBAND

With size S/17mm hook, ch 6.

- Row 1 Work 1 dc in 4th ch from hook (the first 3 ch counts as 1 dc), then in each ch across = 4 dc. Turn.

- Rows 2 - 13 Ch 3 (this counts as 1 dc), work 1 dc in each dc across. Turn.

- Cut yarn and fasten off.

- Weave in yarn ends.

- Sew 1.5"/38mm button at one end (button shown is from designer's stash). Stitches are quite large and button will easily slip through. If you like, you can affix button to neckband with a safety pin, then change the button to suit your mood(s).

plusher red cap

THE CAP

◧◼☐☐ EASY

FINISHED SIZE

- plush cap Approx 20"/51cm around and 7"/18cm deep.
- plusher (red) cap Approx 20"/51cm around and 8"/20cm deep.
- wristlets Approx 8"/20.5cm around and 5.5"/14cm long.

MATERIALS

Muench Yarn Big Baby

(each approx 1.75oz/50g, 100% microfiber acrylic, 50yds/45m)

- 2 balls in color #5508 Reds
- 2 balls in color #5509 Blues (1 ball for cap and 1 ball for wristlets on opposite page)
- One each sizes J/6mm, N/9mm and P/10mm crochet hooks.

GAUGE

- 5 sts and 4 rows to 4"/10cm in double crochet using size P/10mm hook and single strand of of yarn.

Big hook, big yarn, big stitch.
Super-simple pattern.
Instant gratification!

PLUSH CAP

• With size P/10mm hook and single strand yarn, ch 5. Join with slip st to form ring.

• Rnd 1 Ch 3 (this counts as 1 dc in this and every round), then work 11 dc in ring = 12 dc. Slip st to top of first ch-3 to join; do this at end of each round. Do not turn. Continue to work around with the same side always facing you.

• Rnd 2 Ch 3, work 1 dc in same st, then work 2 dc in each dc around = 24 dc.

• Rnd 3 Ch 3, work 1 dc in same st, work 1 dc in each of next 5 dc, [work 2 dc in next dc, work 1 dc in each of next 5 dc] 3 times = 30 dc.

• Rnds 4 - 6 Ch 3, work 1 dc in each st around.

• Cut yarn and fasten off.

• Weave in yarn ends. Use yarn tail to close top of cap.

• Work overcast st around edge.

WRISTLETS

• With size M/9mm hook and single strand of yarn, ch 16.

• Row 1 Work 1 sc in 3rd ch from hook (the first 2 ch counts as 1 sc), then in each ch across = 15 sc. Slip st to top of first ch-2 to form a ring of sc's, being careful not to twist ring.

• Rnd 1 Ch 2 (this counts as 1 sc in this and every round), then working in back loops only, work 1 sc into each sc around.

Slip st to top of first ch-2 to join; do this at end of each round.
Do not turn your work. Continue to work around with the same side facing you.

• Rnds 2 - 6 Rep rnd 1.

• Cut yarn and fasten off.

• Weave in ends. Use yarn tail to sew edges of first row together.

• With length of same or contrast yarn, work overcast st around each edge.

PLUSHER RED CAP

• With size P/10mm hook and 2 strands of yarn held together, ch 5. Join with slip st to form ring.

• Rnd 1 Same as for plush cap.

• Rnd 2 Ch 3, work 1 dc in same st, work 1 dc in next st, *work 2 dc in next st, work 1 dc in next st; repeat from* around = 18 dc.

• Rnds 3 - 5 Ch 3, work 1 dc in each st around.

• Rnd 6 Ch 2, work 1 sc in back loop only of each st around.

• Cut yarn and fasten off.

• Weave in ends. Use yarn tail to close top of cap.

• With 2 strands of yarn held together, work overcast st around edge, working in between sts.

CAMOUFLAGE

(shown on page 100)

■■□□ **EASY**

FINISHED SIZE

• Headband circumference approx 18"/45.5cm

MATERIALS

Noro Taiyo

(each approx 3.5oz/100g, 40% cotton, 30% silk, 15% wool, 15% nylon, 218yds/200m)

• Beret: 1 ball in color #2 Green/Black/Peach

• Wristlets: 1 ball in color #4 Yellow/Rust/Pink

• One each sizes J/6mm and K/6.5mm crochet hooks.

GAUGE

• 12 sts and 6 rows to 4"/10cm in double crochet using size K/6.5mm hook.

"Leave everyone wondering which is the more interesting piece of work ... you or your hat."
—Unknown

BERET

- With size K/6.5mm hook, ch 5. Join with slip st to form ring.

- Rnd 1 Ch 3 (this counts as 1 dc in this and every round), then work 11 dc in ring = 12 dc. Slip st to top of first ch-3 to join; do this at end of each round.
Do not turn your work. Continue around with the same side facing you.

- Rnds 2 - 4 Ch 3, work 1 dc in same stitch, then work 2 dc in each dc around. You are doubling the number of sts in each round = 96 dc.

- Rnds 5 - 10 Ch 3, work 1 dc in each st around.

- Rnd 11 Ch 3, *work 1 dc over next 2 dc as foll: yo, go through st and draw up a loop, yo and through 2 loops (2 loops left on hook), yo again and go through next st and draw up a loop, yo and through 3 loops, yo and through 2 loops on hook, work 1 dc in each of next 2 dc; rep from * around = 72 sts.

- Rnd 12 Ch 3, *work 1 dc over next 2 dc as before, work 1 dc in next dc; rep from* around = 48 dc.

- Rnd 13 Ch 3, then work 1 front post dc in each st around (yo, insert hook from front to back, then to front again around post of dc, complete dc as usual).

- Rnds 14 - 19 With size J/6mm hook, rep rnd 13.

- Rnd 20 Ch 2, work 1 rnd reverse single crochet evenly around.

- Cut yarn and fasten off.

- Weave in yarn ends. Use yarn tail to close top of beret.

WRISTLETS

- With size K/6.5mm hook, ch 24.

- Row 1 Work 1 dc in 4th ch from hook (the first 3 ch counts as 1 dc), then in each ch across = 22 dc. Slip st to top of first ch-3 to form a ring of dc, being careful not to twist ring.

- Rnds 1 - 11 Ch 3 (counts as 1 dc), work 1 dc in each st around. Slip st to top of first ch-3 to join. Do not turn at end of each rnd. Continue around with same side facing you.

- Ruffle Ch 3, *work 2 dc in between each st around. Join with sl st to top of first ch-3.

- Cut yarn and fasten off.

- Weave in yarn ends. Use yarn tail to sew edges of first row together.

PRETTY 'N MAUVE

■■□□ **EASY**

FINISHED SIZE

• Headband circumference approx 17"/43cm

MATERIALS

MEDIUM 4

Tahki Tweedy Alpaca

(each approx 1.75oz/50g, 60% wool, 30% baby alpaca,
7% acrylic, 3% viscose, 81yds/74m)

• 4 balls in color #009 Mauve

The beret alone takes a little over 2 balls.

The wristlets take a little over 1 ball.

4 balls will easily make both.

• One each sizes J/6mm, K/6.5mm and L/8mm crochet hooks.

GAUGE

• 11 sts and 5 rows to 4"/10cm in double crochet using size
L/8mm hook.

Crochet this soft tweed a little loosely

to create a beautifully draped beret.

A smaller hook gives the headband a crisp shape.

BERET

- With size L/8mm hook, ch 5. Join with slip st to form ring.

- Rnd 1 Ch 3 (this counts as 1 dc in this and every round), then work 11 dc in ring = 12 dc. Slip st to top of first ch-3 to join; do this at end of each round. Do not turn your work. Continue around with the same side facing you, working in back loops only of each st to form decorative ridge.

- Rnd 2 Ch 3, work 1 dc in same stitch, then work 2 dc in each dc around = 24 dc.

- Rnd 3 Ch 3, work 1 dc in same stitch, work 1 dc in next dc, *work 2 dc in next dc, work 1 dc in next dc; rep from* around = 36 dc.

- Rnd 4 Ch 3, work 1 dc in same stitch, work 1 dc in each of next 2 dc, *work 2 dc in next dc, work 1 dc in each of next 2 dc; rep from* around = 48 dc.

- Rnd 5 Ch 3, work 1 dc in same stitch, work 1 dc in each of next 3 dc, *work 2 dc in next dc, work 1 dc in each of next 3 dc; rep from* around = 60 dc.

- Rnds 6 - 9 Cont to work as for rnd 5, working 1 more dc in between increases — 4 on rnd 6, 5 on rnd 7, 6 on rnd 8 and 7 on rnd 9 = 108 dc.

Continue to work in back loops only for rnds 10 - 13.

- Rnds 10 and 13 Ch 3, then work 1 dc in each dc around.

- Rnds 11 - 12 Ch 3, *work 1 dc over next 2 dc as foll: yo, go through st and draw up a loop, yo and through 2 loops (2 loops left on hook), yo again and go through next st and draw up a loop, yo and through 3 loops, yo and through 2 loops on hook, work 1 dc in next dc; rep from* around + 48 sts.

- Rnds 14 - 15 With size K/6.5mm hook, ch 3, then work 1 front post dc in each st around (yo, insert hook from front to back, then to front again around post of dc in row below, then complete dc as usual).

- Rnds 16 - 19 With size J/6mm hook, rep rnd 14.

- Rnd 20 Ch 2, work 1 rnd reverse single crochet evenly around.

- Cut yarn and fasten off.

- Weave in yarn ends. Use yarn tail to close top of beret.

WRISTLETS

• With size K/6.5mm hook, ch 24 (or ch 27 for larger wrists).

• Row 1 Work 1 dc in 4th ch from hook (the first 3 ch counts as 1 dc), then in each ch across = 22 dc (or 25 dc for larger size). Slip st to top of first ch-3 to form a ring of dc, being careful not to twist ring.

• Rnd 1 Ch 3 (this counts as 1 dc in this and every round), then working in back loops only, work 1 dc in each dc around = 22 dc (or 25 dc). Slip st to top of first ch-3 to join; do this at end of each round. Do not turn your work. Continue to work around with the same side always facing you.

• Rnds 2-12 Rep rnd 1.

• Ruffle *Ch 5, sc in same st, ch 5, sc in next st; rep from* around, ch 5, sc in same st as first sc.

• Cut yarn and fasten off.

• Weave in yarn ends. Use yarn tail to sew edges of first row together OR leave edge open for more ease.

FINISHED SIZE

• Circumference approx 7"/18cm to fit small to medium sized wrists. Adjustment for larger wrists given in parentheses. Wristlets will stretch.

MATERIALS

See page 99
• Size K/6.5mm crochet hook.

GAUGE

• 12 sts and 6 rows in double crochet to 4"/10cm.

WRAPS

It's too warm outside for a coat, but you still need a little something extra? Throw on a wrap! Lacy shawls, fluffy floral stoles, a fishnet of color pulled from a rainbow sea (dripping with beads, of course!)— these neo-classical wraps to crochet are the icing on your fashion cake. Office to evening. Country getaway. Saunter in the park. Wraps are some of the best ways to show off your personal style!

CITY BLOOMS

■■■□ INTERMEDIATE

FINISHED SIZE

- Wrap measures approx 19"/48.5cm by 60"/152.5cm.
- Each flower motif (before joining) measures approx 3.5"/9cm across.

MATERIALS

Plymouth Yarn® Encore®
(solid color for flower center and joining round)
(each approx 3.5oz/100g, 75% acrylic, 25% wool, 200yds/182m)
- 2 balls in color #960 Purple

Noro Silk Garden Lite
(for smaller, solid color flowers)
(each approx 1.75oz/50g, 45% silk, 45% kid mohair, 10% lambswool, 137yds/125m)
- 2 balls of #2026 denim, grey, camel, sage

Noro Silk Garden
(for round 2 of main flower motif)
(each approx 1.75oz/50g, 45% silk, 45% kid mohair, 10% lambswool, 122yds/111m)
- 1 ball each of 3 different colors:
    #226 grey, blue, purple multi
    #241 purples, greens, rust, blue
    #251 fuschia, magenta, brown, pink, smoke
- One each sizes K/6.5mm and L/8mm crochet hooks.

GAUGE

- 12 sts to 3"/7.5cm in double crochet and Silk Garden using size L/8 mm hook.

WRAP

- Each main motif has a solid color center; then the multi-colored petals are worked.
- The motifs are joined with a solid color fretwork.
- The small, round flowers are worked in between the motifs after the larger motifs are joined.
- A solid color border is then added, followed by a multi-colored picot edge.

MAIN FLOWER MOTIF (MAKE A TOTAL OF 48 MOTIFS)

One ball of Silk Garden will make 16 flowers. You can join as you go (round 3), choosing to work from one ball at a time or making flowers from separate balls. OR you can make the 48 motifs, lay them out as you wish and then join the motifs (round 3).

CLUSTER

In same ch-1 sp, work [yo, insert hook into sp and pull up a loop, yo and pull through 2 lps] 3 times, yo and pull through all 4 lps on hook.

- With solid color and size K/6.5mm hook, ch 5, join with sl st to form ring.

- Rnd 1 Ch 4, work [1 dc in ring, ch 1] 11 times, slip st to 3rd ch of first ch-4 = 12 ch-1 spaces.

- Cut yarn and fasten off. Do not turn motif.

- Rnd 2 With size L/8 mm hook, join Silk Garden multi-color to any ch-1 sp, ch 3, [yo, insert hook in same sp and pull up a loop, yo and pull through 2 lps] twice, yo and pull through all 3 lps on hook; then [ch 3, work Cluster] in each ch-1 sp around, end ch 3, slip st to top of first ch-3.

- Cut yarn and fasten off.

- Rnd 3 With RS facing, solid color and size K/6.5mm hook, join yarn to any ch-3 sp, ch 5,* sc in next sp, ch 5; rep from * around, slip st to first st of first ch-5.

- Cut yarn and fasten off.

TO JOIN MOTIFS ON ROUND 3

- On 2nd motif, join yarn and work first 2 ch-5s of rnd 3, then *ch 2, slip st in any ch-5 sp of first motif (inserting hook from the top in the ch-5 sp), ch 2, then sc in next ch-3 sp; rep from* twice, then complete rnd 3 = 3 ch-5 sps of 2 motifs joined.

- In same way, use photo as guide and join motifs, forming rows 12 motifs long by 4 motifs wide.

In the photo, the large flowers look as if they are joined with a solid line of color between the 4 long rows. In fact, all the main motifs are joined with the same ch–5 fretwork.

SMALL JOINING FLOWERS (33 IN ALL)

• In the photo above, the small yellow flower in the top row, 4th from left, clearly shows how you are joining the flower to the 8 ch-5 spaces of the 4 larger flowers. Work with the right side facing you throughout.

• I chose to work the small flowers with the lengths of bright color within Silk Garden Lite. Wrap the darker colors into a ball to use in the picot border.

• With size K/6.5mm hook and Silk Garden Lite, ch 5. Join with slip st to form ring.

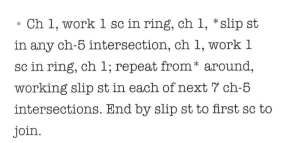

- Ch 1, work 1 sc in ring, ch 1, *slip st in any ch-5 intersection, ch 1, work 1 sc in ring, ch 1; repeat from* around, working slip st in each of next 7 ch-5 intersections. End by slip st to first sc to join.

- Cut yarn and fasten off.

BORDER

- With size K/6.5 hook and solid color, join yarn to any ch-5 space, ch 2, work 4 sc into same space; then continue to work 5 sc in each ch-5 space around. Where two flowers join, work 3 sc in each partial ch-5 space. Slip st to first ch-2 to join.

- Cut yarn and fasten off.

PICOT EDGE

- With size K/6.5 hook, Silk Garden Lite and working in back loops only, ch 1, *slip st in 3 sts, ch 3, make picot by slip st in first ch; repeat from* around. Slip st to first ch-1 to join.

- Cut yarn and fasten off.

- Block piece lightly.

PARK PLACE WRAP

◖■◗☐☐ **EASY +**

FINISHED SIZE

• Approx 44"/112cm square after blocking.

MATERIALS

Skacel Zitron Trekking Hand Art

(each skein 3.5oz/100g, 75% superwash wool, 25% polyamid, 462yds/420m)

• (A) 1 skein in #511 Tobago
• (B) 1 skein in #512 Trinidad
• Size G/4mm crochet hook.
• Optional: Assorted plastic beads, each 4mm to 6mm.

Beading 2 sides of the wrap took approx 56 beads; beading 4 sides would take about 112 beads.

GAUGE

• 18 sts to 4"/10cm in double crochet using size G/4mm hook.

Use this gauge as a guide. Work a long chain. If you feel comfortable with your hook size and yarn, not too tight, not too loose, you will be fine. The yarn is crocheted looser than normal to achieve a desired drape. Once the piece is washed, it will open up even more.

WRAP

- With size G/4mm crochet hook and color A, ch 5. Join with slip st to form ring.

- Rnd 1 *Ch 5, sc in ring; repeat from* 7 times more = 8 ch-5 loops.

- Rnd 2 Slip st in next loop, *ch 5, sc in same loop, (ch 5, sc in next loop) twice; repeat from* 3 times, end by working final sc in first ch-5 loop.

- Rnd 3 *Ch 5, sc in same loop (corner), (ch 5, sc in next loop) 3 times; rep from * around, end by working sc in first corner.

- Rnds 4 - 16 Rep rnd 3 increasing one ch-5 between corners each rnd.
You can also count the "corners" along the diagonal. Just end at your marked corner.

Continue in pattern and work in color stripes as follows:
- 5 rnds of Color B
- 7 rnds of Color A
- 5 rnds of Color B
- 9 rnds of Color A
- 7 rnds of Color B.

- Cut yarn and fasten off.

BEADS (OPTIONAL)

I beaded one side of the wrap at a time. Since the beads need to be on the yarn while crocheting, I found it awkward and time-consuming to keep pushing, then pulling them into position. Working with fewer rather than more beads was easier for me. It also saves wear and tear on the yarn.

- Thread enough beads (approx 28) onto yarn to crochet 1 side.

- Join yarn to a corner and ch 2, slide bead up to crochet hook and ch around it, ch 2, sc in next loop. Ch 5, sc in next sp, then join a bead as before in the following ch-5 sp. Continue to join beads to the wrap every other space until you reach another corner. Cut yarn and fasten off. Bead each side as desired.

- Wrap as shown has 2 consecutive sides with beads.

- Join a bead into consecutive spaces around the corners or join a bead into every space. The more beads you use, the more weight you will give to the wrap.

FINISHING

Hand wash wrap in cold water. I used a splash of Ivory dish detergent. Rinse carefully and squeeze out as much excess moisture as possible. Lay flat to dry.
When dry, weave in ends.

Here's a variation of
Park Place Wrap.
Using just one skein of yarn, it's
beaded all around and measures
about 34"/86.5 cm square.
It's your new go-to accessory!

BEADS ALL AROUND VERSION

▮▮▢▢ EASY +

MATERIALS

Skacel Zitron Trekking Hand Art

(each skein 3.5oz/100g, 75% superwash wool, 25% polyamid, 462yds/420m)

• 1 skein in #501 Fire

• Size G/4mm crochet hook.

• Optional: Approx 150 assorted plastic beads, each 4mm to 6mm. Each side took approx 37 beads.

GAUGE

• See gauge for Park Place Wrap (page 115).

WRAP

• Follow the pattern for Park Place Wrap (page 116), working a total of 36 rounds.

• When working beads, work a bead in every ch-5 instead of every other ch-5.

SIMPLY WRAPPED

◖■☐☐ **EASY**

FINISHED SIZE

• Approx 20"/51cm by 94"/239cm, including ruffled border.

MATERIALS

Red Heart® Collage™

(each skein 3.5oz/100g, 100% acrylic, 218yds/200m)

• 2 skeins in #2407 Ice Storm
• 2 skeins in #2934 Tundra
• One each sizes K/6.5mm and P/10mm crochet hook.

GAUGE

• 16 sts and 5 rows to 4"/10cm in double crochet using size K/6.5mm hook.

Use this gauge as a guide. The piece will "fit" even if you are not getting the exact gauge.

"The way you overcome shyness is to become so wrapped up in something that you forget to be afraid."

– Lady Bird Johnson

WRAP

• With size K/6.5mm hook and Tundra, ch 296.

• Work 1 dc in 4th ch from hook, *ch 1, skip 1 ch, 1 dc in next ch; rep from * across, end with 1 dc in final ch. If you have to leave a few sts to rip back later, that's OK. You can work the pattern row as long as you end with ch 1, 1 dc. Turn.

• Row 1 Ch 3, 1 dc in ch-1 sp, *ch 1, 1 dc in next ch-1 sp; repeat from* across, end with ch 1, work final dc in between last 2 sts. Turn.

• Repeat row 1 and work through yarn as follows: work through entire skein of Tundra, then Ice Storm, then Tundra. Work through final skein of Ice Storm until piece measures approx 18"/45.5cm from beginning.

• Cut yarn and fasten off.

RUFFLED BORDER

• With size P/10mm hook, join yarn to any ch-1 sp along long edge, *ch 3, sc in same sp, ch 3, sc in next sp; repeat from * around.

• At each side (short) edge, I chose to work *ch 3, sc in same sp, ch 3, skip next intersection (which contains the 2 dc); repeat from* across. You can work more or less ruffles as you wish along the short edge.

A TOUCH OF VENUS

 EASY

FINISHED SIZE

- Approx 53"/134.5cm along center of triangle
(from neck to lower point of V, measured flat)
- Approx 114"/289.5cm across top of triangle (57"/145cm
from center back neck to one end of triangle)
- Measurements are taken after blocking
(see finishing). The piece definitely hangs longer when
worn, a good 3"/7.5cm - 4"/10cm.

MATERIALS

S. Charles Collezione Venus **MEDIUM 4**

(each ball 1.75oz/50g, 95% viscose, 5% polyamid,
83yds/75m)
- 1 ball each in the following colors:
  - #60 Orchid/Blue/Fuschia
  - #38 Lavender/Pink
  - #07 Black/Brights Multi
  - #23 Brown/Purple/Green/Orange
  - #68 Jewel Tone Multi
  - #52 Rainshow Sherbet Multi
  - #49 Red/Brown/Green/Gold/Blue
  - #57 Bright Pastel Multi
  - #48 Brown/Blue/Gold
  - #54 Pink/Orange/Purple
- Size J/6mm crochet hook.
- Optional: Dritz® Fray Check™

GAUGE

- 16 sts to 4"/10cm in double crochet using size J/6mm hook.

- Work up a small piece in double crochet and do not cut yarn (you can unravel this piece to use in the wrap). Put a safety pin through the final, open stitch.

- Hand wash the piece in the sink, then lay it flat to dry. If the piece is not too tight, not too loose, you will be fine. If it's a little loose, that's all right. The yarn is crocheted looser than normal, then hand-washed to achieve a desired drape.

NOTES

- This wrap begins at center top of the triangle which corresponds to the neck edge. The colors are used in the order listed in the materials section, beginning with #60 (neck edge) and continuing through #54 (lower edge of triangle).

- Think of the colors as beginning with dark, then a bright color, then dark, then bright and so forth, ending with a bright color.

- Work through each ball of color until it's done. I joined the new color, even if I was in the middle of a row. Because of the number of vibrant colors used and the way the piece drapes, it's difficult for the human eye to distinguish where the colors begin and end in a row.

WRAP

- With size J/6mm crochet hook and first color, ch 6. Join with slip st to form ring.

- Row 1 Ch 3, work 2 dc in ring, [ch 3, work 3 dc in ring] twice. Turn.

- Row 2 [Ch 5, sc in ch-3 sp, ch 3, sc in same sp] twice, ch 5, sc in top of first ch-3. Turn.

- Row 3 Ch 3, work (2 dc, ch 2, 2 dc) in first ch-5 sp, ch 3, sc in ch-3 sp, ch 3, work (3 dc, ch 2, 3 dc) in ch-5 sp, ch 3, sc in ch-3 sp, ch 3, work (2 dc, ch 2, 2 dc) in final ch-5 sp. Turn.

- Row 4 Ch 3, work (2 dc, ch 2, 2 dc) in ch-2 sp, [ch 3, sc in next ch-3 sp] twice, ch 4, work (3 dc, ch 2, 3 dc) in next ch-2 sp, ch 4, sc in next ch-3 sp, ch 3, sc in next ch-3 sp, ch 3, work (2 dc, ch 2, 2 dc) in final ch-2 sp. Turn.

- Row 5 Ch 3, work (2 dc, ch 2, 2 dc) in ch-2 sp, [ch 3, sc in next ch-3 sp] twice, ch 3, sc in ch-4 sp, ch 4, work (3 dc, ch 2, 3 dc) in next ch-2 sp (this is center of V), ch 4, sc in next ch-4 sp, [ch 3, sc in next ch-3 sp] twice, ch 3, work (2 dc, ch 2, 2 dc) in final ch-2 sp. Turn.

- Row 6 Ch 3, work (2 dc, ch 2, 2 dc) in ch-2 sp, [ch 3, sc in next sp] across to center of V, ch 4, work (3 dc, ch 2, 3 dc) in next ch-2 sp, ch 4, [sc in next sp, ch 3] across, work (2 dc, ch 2, 2 dc) in final ch-2 sp. Turn.

- Repeat row 6, working through all 9 colors. You can end the 9th color at one edge OR work as much as you can of a row with the 9th color (which is what I did) and tie on the 10th color, then finish the row.

- Final row Ch 3, work (2 dc, ch 2, 2 dc) in ch-2 sp, *ch 4, sc in next ch-3 sp, ch 3, sc in same sp; repeat from* across entire piece, ending ch 4, work (2 dc, ch 2, 2 dc) in final ch-2 sp.

- Cut yarn and fasten off.

- Weave in ends. If desired, use a liquid seam sealant on yarn ends. Because of the yarn construction, the fibers have a tendency to "butterfly" or fray at the ends. You can also dab clear nail polish or a mild, white household glue on the ends. Use a cotton swab to apply sparingly.

FINISHING

Hand wash wrap in cold water in sink. I used a splash of Ivory dish detergent. Rinse carefully and squeeze out as much excess moisture as possible. Lay flat to dry. When dry, re-weave ends if necessary.

GENERAL INSTRUCTIONS

ABBREVIATIONS

approx	approximately
ch(s)	chain(s)
cm	centimeters
cont	continue
dc	double crochet(s)
FPdc	Front Post double crochet(s)
FPdctog	Front Post double crochet decrease
hdc	half double crochet(s)
lps	loops
mm	millimeters
rep	repeat
Rnd(s)	Round(s)
RS	right side
sc	single crochet(s)
sp(s)	space(s)
st(s)	stitch(es)
tog	together
tr	treble crochet(s)
yo	yarn over

* — work instructions following * as many **more** times as indicated in addition to the first time.

( ) or **[ ]** — work enclosed instructions as many times as specified by the number immediately following **or** work all enclosed instructions in the stitch or space indicated **or** contains explanatory remarks.

= — the number(s) given after an equals sign at the end of a row or round denote(s) the number of stitches you should have on that row or round.

GAUGE

Exact gauge is essential for proper fit. Before beginning your project, make the sample swatch given in the individual instructions in the yarn and hook specified. After completing the swatch, measure it, counting your stitches and rows carefully. If your swatch is larger or smaller than specified, make another, **changing hook size to get the correct gauge**. Keep trying until you find the size hook that will give you the specified gauge. Once proper gauge is obtained, measure width of garment approximately every 3" (7.5 cm) to be sure gauge remains consistent.

CROCHET TERMINOLOGY

UNITED STATES		INTERNATIONAL
slip stitch (slip st)	=	single crochet (sc)
single crochet (sc)	=	double crochet (dc)
half double crochet (hdc)	=	half treble crochet (htr)
double crochet (dc)	=	treble crochet (tr)
treble crochet (tr)	=	double treble crochet (dtr)
double treble crochet (dtr)	=	triple treble crochet (ttr)
triple treble crochet (tr tr)	=	quadruple treble crochet (qtr)
skip	=	miss

Yarn Weight Symbol & Names	SUPER FINE 1	FINE 2	LIGHT 3	MEDIUM 4	BULKY 5	SUPER BULKY 6
Type of Yarns in Category	Sock, Fingering Baby	Sport, Baby	DK, Light Worsted	Worsted, Afghan, Aran	Chunky, Craft, Rug	Bulky, Roving
Crochet Gauge Ranges in Single Crochet to 4" (10 cm)	21-32 sts	16-20 sts	12-17 sts	11-14 sts	8-11 sts	5-9 sts
Advised Hook Size Range	B-1 to E-4	E-4 to 7	7 to I-9	I-9 to K-10.5	K-10.5 to M-13	M-13 and larger

CROCHET HOOKS

U.S.	B-1	C-2	D-3	E-4	F-5	G-6	H-8	I-9	J-10	K-10$\frac{1}{2}$	L	N	P	Q	S
Metric - mm	2.25	2.75	3.25	3.5	3.75	4	5	5.5	6	6.5	8	9	10	15	19

■□□□ BEGINNER	Projects for first-time crocheters using basic stitches. Minimal shaping.
■■□□ EASY	Projects using yarn with basic stitches, repetitive stitch patterns, simple color changes, and simple shaping and finishing.
■■■□ INTERMEDIATE	Projects using a variety of techniques, such as basic lace patterns or color patterns, mid-level shaping and finishing.
■■■■ EXPERIENCED	Projects with intricate stitch patterns, techniques and dimension, such as non-repeating patterns, multi-color techniques, fine threads, small hooks, detailed shaping and refined finishing.

POST STITCH

Work around post of stitch indicated, inserting hook in direction of arrow (**Fig. 1**).

Fig. 1

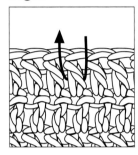

WORKING IN SPACE BEFORE A STITCH

When instructed to work in space before a stitch or in spaces between stitches, insert hook in space indicated by arrow (**Fig. 2**).

Fig. 2

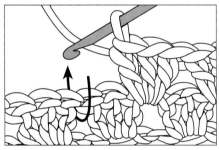

BACK LOOP ONLY

Work only in loop indicated by arrow (**Fig. 3**).

Fig. 3

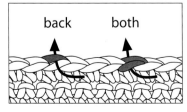

REVERSE SINGLE CROCHET (ABBREVIATED REVERSE SC)

Working from left to right, ★ insert hook in st to right of hook (**Fig. 4a**), YO and draw through, under and to left of loop on hook (2 loops on hook) (**Fig. 4b**), YO and draw through both loops on hook (**Fig. 4c**) (**reverse sc made, Fig. 4d**); repeat from ★ across or around.

Fig. 4a

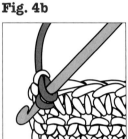

Fig. 4b

Fig. 4c

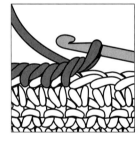

Fig. 4d

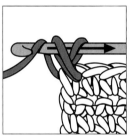